Thinking Machines

Exploring AI's Present and Future

By

Altaf Siddiqui, PhD

Greg Jameson

If you want help implementing any of the ideas in this book, please schedule a time to talk with the authors at

Altaf Siddiqui: Amer.Entps@gmail.com

Greg Jameson: greg@gregjameson.com

Legal Notice

The information contained in this book is for information purposes only and may not apply to your situation. The author, publisher, and distributor provide no warranty about the content or accuracy of content enclosed.

Neither the Publisher or Author shall be liable for any loss of profit or other commercial damages resulting from use of this guide.

No part of this book may be reproduced, stored in a retrieval system, or transmitted in any form or by any means—electronic, mechanical, photocopying, recording, or otherwise—without prior written permission from the publisher, except for brief quotations used in critical reviews or articles.

Trademarks and Copyrights

All trademarks and copyrights mentioned herein remain the property of their respective owners. No part of this work should be interpreted as endorsing or infringing upon any trademarks or copyrights. All references are for educational or parody purposes, used under Nominative Fair Use.

Published by WebStores Ltd.
ISBN-13: 978-0-9991727-2-8

"Dr. Altaf Siddiqui and Greg Jameson have fed their passion of sharing knowledge by demystifying the complexities of Artificial Intelligence. Their combined expertise, deep academic and instructional background in IT and emerging technologies, and extensive experience in AI-driven business innovation brings a well-rounded and practical perspective to the subject. Their ability to break down intricate AI concepts into relatable, real-world applications is commendable. This book not only provides a clear understanding of AI fundamentals but also offers valuable guidance to entrepreneurs, professionals, and learners seeking to navigate the AI landscape effectively. Anyone looking to harness AI's transformative potential in both technical and strategic capacities, must read this book."

-- Asif Allauddin, PMP, MBA, MIS & Finance
Vice President & Head of Global Delivery at Tectonic
LLC

"Artificial Intelligence is no longer a futuristic fantasy, but a present reality shaping every facet of our lives. In "Thinking Machines: Exploring AI's Present and Future", Greg and Altaf provide a timely and essential exploration of this rapidly evolving field. They navigate the intricacies *of Machine Learning and Deep Learning while examining AI's impact on everyday life, healthcare, and the future impact on Employment due to AI and Automation. They also tackle critical Ethical considerations and biases that arise in AI Development, while also offering a forward-looking outlook on its future and market trends.*

I was enlightened by Greg and Altaf's clear and engaging journey into the age of Intelligent Machines, empowering many like myself to navigate the present and shape the future of AI."

-- Waheed Abdul, Executive Director, AI & Innovation, TTEC Digital

"Artificial intelligence is no longer a concept of the future—it's here, shaping the way we work, shop, communicate, and make decisions. Thinking Machines: Exploring AI's Present and Future is designed to help you, and the everyday individuals and entrepreneurs navigate the complex and ever-changing AI landscape with clarity and confidence. Whether you are curious about how AI influences your daily life or looking to integrate it into your profession, or business strategy, this book breaks down key concepts into accessible, real-world insights.

*From fundamental AI principles—such as machine
learning, generative AI, deep learning, and data-driven
decision-making—to its role in automation, decision-
making, and competitive business strategies, this book
guides and explores both the opportunities and challenges
of AI adoption. Through practical examples and expert
analysis and questions, readers will gain a deep
appreciation for how AI is reshaping industries, lives, jobs,
and society. With an eye on ethical concerns, AI
limitations, and future market trends, I
recommend Thinking Machines as it empowers readers to
make informed decisions, harness AI's potential, and stay
ahead in an AI-driven and advancing world."*

**--Dr. Khalid Mansour, AI Strategy and Transformation
Leader,
School of Pharmacy,
Anschutz Medical Campus, Aurora, Colorado**

*"Thinking Machines" is an essential roadmap for anyone
navigating the evolving landscape of AI. Siddiqui and
Jameson expertly break down complex concepts, making
them accessible to both technical and non-technical
audiences. The book's blend of practical examples, ethical
considerations, and future trends provides a holistic
understanding of AI's transformative power. This is a must-*

read for anyone looking to harness AI's potential and stay *ahead in an AI-driven world.*

Kimberly Reynolds,
Co-Founder
AIAdvantageAgency.com

AI is reshaping the world, and Thinking Machines *is the perfect intro for anyone looking to understand it. This book breaks down AI's history, key types, and real-world impact—especially how small businesses can use it to compete.*

The authors highlight why learning AI is essential, how it's transforming jobs, and the critical role of human-created data. Clear and insightful, Thinking Machines *is a must-read for anyone wanting to stay ahead in the AI era.*

- Samuel A. Helms, PhD.
Ai Coach and leading educational technologist
beaconlearningai.com

CONTENTS

FORWARD

THINKING MACHINES: EXPLORING AI'S PRESENT AND FUTURE

In a world that is rapidly advancing, where the boundaries between human capability and technological innovation continue to blur, understanding the essence and scope of artificial intelligence (AI) and machine learning (ML) has never been more crucial. This book serves as a vital primer, ushering readers into the fascinating world of AI, from its foundational theories to the cutting-edge applications that define our daily lives and sculpt our future, we are invited to navigate this dynamic field with both enthusiasm and critical awareness.

As a lifelong learner and educator, I am particularly excited about how AI can enhance educational experiences, creating personalized learning environments that adapt to individual needs. Yet, as we advance, we must proceed with a conscientious framework that prioritizes ethical considerations, ensuring that AI serves humanity with fairness and respect.

AI's potential to tailor learning experiences to individual needs, automate administrative tasks, and provide real-time feedback presents unprecedented opportunities for educators and learners alike. Yet, this integration is not without challenges. It demands a deep understanding of both the technological capabilities of AI and the pedagogical principles that underpin effective teaching. This book brings together leading experts Dr. Altaf Siddiqui and Greg Jameson to deliver insights into how AI can be harnessed to support and enhance instructional design.

This book is not just an academic discourse but a call to action. It encourages the adoption of AI in thoughtful, informed, and innovative ways to not only enhance the delivery of education but also to inspire continual improvement in the field of instructional design. It is an essential read for those seeking to understand, not just what AI is, but what it can be and should be in a world where technology and humanity increasingly intersect.

Whether you are a student, a professional, or a curious mind, the knowledge in this book will equip you with a robust understanding and critical perspective on one of the most significant technologies in recent history.

AUTHORS:

Dr. Altaf Siddiqui is a seasoned IT expert with over two decades of experience in diverse IT roles, including as an adjunct professor, inventor of an Instructional Modeling Language in

Educational Technology, and a Senior/Master Trainer teaching a wide range of subjects like Java, Python, and AI.

Greg Jameson is known as "the AI Architect for Business Growth," with over three decades of experience in transforming business operations online through the evolution of ecommerce and artificial intelligence, guiding both entrepreneurs and corporations to harness technology for growth.

By Dr. Rebecca M. Reese – Director of Online Learning, Rocky Mountain College of Art and Design.

WHAT TO EXPECT FROM THIS BOOK?

AI is a widely discussed topic, and many people feel confused. While IT professionals make it sound straightforward, non-IT people often feel overwhelmed by what they should learn and what will benefit them most. The authors of this book have provided a comprehensive comparison of AI tools and technologies, along with recommendations for the public and entrepreneurs to maximize the benefits of AI. For end users, we hope our recommendations help you make informed decisions about what to learn to simplify your work and save time. For entrepreneurs and project managers, this book aims to guide you in making informed strategic decisions to find your niche and increase revenue. We invite you to contact us in either case and to share your journey and success stories.

CHAPTER 1: WHAT IS MACHINE LEARNING AND ARTIFICIAL INTELLIGENCE (AI)?

Definitions and Core Concepts:

Before diving into Machine Learning (ML), it is essential to grasp the essence of Artificial Intelligence (AI). AI encompasses the development of hardware and software that emulate human intelligence, making it "artificial" due to its non-human nature. Sometimes, it is just software, and other times it could be a combination. A robot's physical outlook is not the defining factor; rather, it is the software within the robot that makes it behave like a human being. Many software solutions qualify as AI because of their ability to perform like humans. AI replicates cognitive functions such as learning, problem-solving, and decision-making. The core strength of AI lies in its capacity to undertake tasks traditionally requiring human intelligence, which has become a pivotal aspect of modern technology.

In daily life, AI is all around us, seamlessly integrated into activities without our explicit recognition. From voice-activated assistants like Siri and Alexa to recommendation systems on streaming platforms and shopping sites, AI's practical uses continue to expand. These systems improve by learning from user behavior, showcasing AI's dynamic and adaptive nature.

Unlike historical technological advancements, such as the invention of the wheel or the automobile, AI's transformative impact extends beyond enhancing physical capabilities. These earlier inventions revolutionized transportation and efficiency, but AI enhances intellectual tasks, pushing the boundaries of what is possible.

Focusing on the contemporary understanding of AI, we see advanced technologies that have revolutionized various fields. Machine Learning (ML), a subset of AI, uses software to implement algorithms through programming languages like Python, Java, and others. For smaller datasets, the existing CPUs will work. At the same time, advanced hardware is required to support complex ML problems, such as Graphic Processing Units (GPUs) and Neuromorphic computer chips. The software solutions used in ML address specific problems within domains such as voice recognition, medical imaging, and more. Since there are algorithms to solve problems in almost every domain, Machine Learning is a constantly growing phenomenon. This is one reason that ML will be used in almost every industry. It is just a matter of time before ML is incorporated into every business, where tasks can be automated and costs can be saved.

Within ML, Neural Networks (NNs)—algorithms inspired by the structure and function of neurons in the human brain—play a significant role. NNs fall into the deep learning category, which is a subset of ML. The development of NNs has led to breakthroughs in healthcare, where algorithms assist in diagnosing diseases, and in finance, where they predict market trends. AI's transformative impact is underscored by its ability to handle vast amounts of data, uncovering patterns and insights beyond human capacity. This is crucial in today's data-driven world, where information overload is a common issue. AI's prowess in data analysis and pattern recognition enables informed decision-making and opens new avenues for innovation and problem-solving. This is another area of growth where NNs learn from their iterations, much like how humans learn. Here again, the sky is the limit when it comes to the diversity of problem domains and their solutions using NNs. The relationship between AI, ML, and DL is shown in Figure 1.

Not every Machine Learning problem is best suited for a Neural Network, though neural networks are highly versatile and capable of addressing a wide range of problems. The suitability of a neural network depends on the nature of the problem, the characteristics of the data, and the computational resources available.

Problems Where Neural Networks Shine

HIGH-DIMENSIONAL DATA:

Neural networks excel in processing large, high-dimensional datasets, such as images, audio, and text due to their ability to learn complex patterns and features from the data. This capability makes them particularly effective for tasks like image classification, where they can identify objects such as cats in photos by recognizing intricate visual details. Similarly, in natural language processing tasks, neural networks can translate languages by understanding the context and semantics of the text. Their layered structure allows for the extraction of higher-level features from raw data, enabling them to perform these tasks with remarkable accuracy and efficiency. These strengths make neural networks a powerful tool in many modern AI applications.

COMPLEX RELATIONSHIPS:

Neural networks are particularly powerful for tasks where the relationship between features and labels is highly non-linear, enabling them to handle complex datasets with intricate patterns. For instance, in autonomous driving, neural networks integrate and process multiple sensor inputs, such as cameras and radar, to predict actions. This requires the network to understand and manage the non-linear relationships between different data sources to make real-time driving decisions. By learning from vast amounts of driving data, neural networks can identify subtle correlations and interactions that traditional algorithms might miss, thereby enhancing the vehicle's ability to navigate safely and efficiently. This capability makes neural networks indispensable in scenarios requiring high adaptability and precision.

Neural Networks have a unique capability to handle unstructured data effectively. When faced with unstructured data, humans might find it difficult to discern any meaningful patterns or relationships simply by looking at it. This is where Neural Networks come into play. They can employ algorithms such as k-means clustering to organize data based on their distance from a central point, known as the centroid or autoencoders using Neural Networks. This clustering process groups data points with similar characteristics, much like bees swarming around honey. These clusters form groups of data that share common features.

Once the data is clustered, subject matter experts can then analyze these groups to extract valuable insights and make well-founded interpretations. For instance, in the marketing domain, customer data is often vast and unstructured. Neural Networks can cluster this data to identify distinct customer segments, enabling businesses to customize their marketing strategies for different target audiences more effectively. In the healthcare sector, clustering algorithms can be used to group patients based on their medical history and symptoms, facilitating more personalized treatment plans.

Moreover, the clustering capability of Neural Networks can be extended to various fields such as finance, where they can detect patterns in transaction data to identify fraudulent activities, or in social media analysis, where they can group users based on their behavior and preferences. The power of Neural Networks lies in their ability to manage unstructured data and form meaningful clusters, providing a robust tool for analyzing complex datasets and uncovering hidden patterns. This ability not only enhances data interpretation but also aids in decision-making processes across different industries.

Overall, Neural Networks offer a significant advantage in handling unstructured data, making them an asset in the modern data-driven world source.

Problems Where Neural Networks Are Suboptimal

SMALL DATASETS:

Neural networks require large datasets to learn effectively due to their complex architectures and vast number of parameters. When trained on small datasets, neural networks are prone to overfitting, which means they learn the noise in the training data rather than the underlying patterns. This leads to poor generalization on new, unseen data. In contrast, simpler models like linear regression or decision trees are better suited for small datasets. For example, predicting house prices using a dataset with only 100 samples is more efficiently handled by linear regression or decision trees, as these models are less likely to overfit and can still capture the essential relationships between features and the target variable without the need for extensive data.

SIMPLE RELATIONSHIPS:

When the data exhibits a clear, interpretable linear or polynomial relationship, simpler models such as linear regression or support vector machines (SVMs) are preferable due to their straightforward implementation and interpretability. These models can effectively capture the underlying trends without the risk of overfitting, which is a common issue with more complex models like neural networks, especially with smaller datasets. For instance, in modeling the relationship between hours studied and exam scores, a linear regression model can efficiently determine the direct correlation between the two variables, providing a simple yet powerful way to predict exam performance based on study hours. This approach not only offers clarity in understanding the data but also ensures robust and reliable predictions without unnecessary complexity.

SPARSE AND TABULAR DATA:

Algorithms like Gradient Boosted Trees, such as XGBoost and LightGBM, often outperform neural networks when it comes to structured, tabular datasets due to their ability to efficiently handle numerical and categorical features without extensive preprocessing. These algorithms excel in capturing intricate patterns and interactions between features through an ensemble of decision trees, making them particularly powerful for predictive tasks. For example, in predicting loan defaults using tabular financial data, Gradient Boosted Trees can effectively model the complex relationships between various financial indicators and the likelihood of default. They provide robust and interpretable results, which are essential for making informed decisions in the financial industry. Their superior performance on structured data makes them a go-to choice for many machine learning practitioners.

PROBABILISTIC MODELING:

Problems that require explicit probability outputs or make specific assumptions about data distributions are often best handled by probabilistic models such as Naive Bayes or Gaussian Mixture Models. These models excel in scenarios where understanding the likelihood of different outcomes is crucial, as they inherently provide probabilistic predictions. For instance, in the task of classifying emails as spam or not, Naive Bayes is particularly effective. This model operates under the assumption that the words in an email are independent, making it computationally efficient while still achieving high accuracy. By calculating the probability of an email being spam based on the presence of certain words, Naive Bayes provides clear, interpretable probabilistic outputs that aid in decision-making. This capability makes probabilistic models highly valuable in various domains where uncertainty and probability play a key role.

LIMITED COMPUTATIONAL RESOURCES:

Neural networks, especially deep learning models, can be computationally expensive, demanding substantial resources for both training and inference. This high computational cost often necessitates powerful hardware, such as GPUs and TPUs, and considerable amounts of energy. A Tensor Processing Unit (TPU) is a specialized hardware accelerator developed by Google to optimize and accelerate the execution of machine learning tasks, particularly those involving deep learning and neural networks. As a result, deploying these models in environments with limited computational resources, like edge devices, can be challenging. Edge devices, which operate with low power and limited processing capability, may instead rely on simpler models for real-time predictions. For instance, in applications like real-time object detection on smartphones or IoT devices, lightweight models such as decision trees or linear classifiers are often preferred. These models can efficiently operate within the constraints of edge devices, providing timely and accurate predictions without overwhelming the available resources.

Why Some Problems Can't Be Done with Neural Networks

Neural networks are universal function approximators, meaning they can theoretically learn any function given enough data and computational power.

Some problems are best addressed using exact mathematical methods rather than approximations, making neural networks unnecessary for such tasks. For instance, solving linear equations or determining the shortest path in a graph can be efficiently handled using precise algorithms and mathematical techniques. Linear equations can be solved using matrix operations or Gaussian elimination, providing exact solutions without the need for iterative training. Similarly, graph algorithms like Dijkstra's or the Floyd-Warshall algorithm can accurately compute the shortest paths between nodes, leveraging clear mathematical principles. These methods offer exact, reliable results with minimal computational overhead, highlighting the importance of choosing the right approach for specific problem types.

FEATURE ENGINEERING DOMINANCE:

In certain domains, hand-crafted features grounded in domain-specific knowledge can significantly outperform neural networks by leveraging established expertise and insights. For example, in epidemiology, calculating risk scores based on predefined clinical guidelines allows for precise and reliable assessments that align with medical standards. These hand-crafted features, derived from rigorous clinical research and guidelines, provide a level of accuracy and interpretability that neural networks might struggle to achieve without extensive and specialized training data. This approach ensures that risk scores are not only accurate but also transparent and justifiable, which is crucial in healthcare settings where decision-making impacts patient outcomes and must adhere to established protocols.

INTERPRETABILITY REQUIREMENTS:

Many domains, such as healthcare and finance, necessitate the use of interpretable models for reasons of trust and regulatory compliance. In these fields, the ability to understand and explain the decision-making process is crucial, as it ensures that the models' predictions can be trusted and verified. Neural networks, which often function as "black boxes" due to their complex and opaque nature, may not meet these stringent requirements. For instance, when predicting patient outcomes in a clinical trial, healthcare professionals need to understand the factors influencing the model's predictions to ensure they align with clinical knowledge and ethical standards. Transparent models, such as logistic regression or decision trees, offer clear insights into how predictions are made, facilitating better decision-making and compliance with regulatory guidelines. This need for interpretability underscores the importance of choosing the right model for specific applications where trust and accountability are paramount.

Key Takeaway

While neural networks are extremely versatile, they are not a one-size-fits-all solution. The choice of a machine learning algorithm depends on:

- The size and nature of the dataset.

- The problem's complexity.

- Computational and time constraints.

- The need for interpretability or explainability.

In many cases, simpler models like linear regression, decision trees, or probabilistic models are faster, more interpretable, and sufficient for the task at hand.

Neural networks, especially deep learning models, are particularly well-suited for handling unstructured data such as raw images, audio, and text. These models excel in extracting complex features from raw inputs, allowing them to make sense of data that lacks a clear, predefined structure. For example, in speech recognition, deep learning models analyze raw waveforms to identify patterns and features that correspond to different phonemes and words. By learning from large datasets, these models can effectively interpret the nuances of human speech, including accents and intonations, resulting in highly accurate transcriptions. This ability to process and understand unstructured data makes neural networks invaluable in applications ranging from image and video analysis to natural language processing and beyond.

In summary, AI, with its ability to emulate human intelligence and perform complex tasks, is a cornerstone of modern technology. Its journey from simple algorithms to advanced systems highlights its growing significance and potential. As AI technologies continue to evolve, the line between human and artificial intelligence will blur further, ushering in an era of unprecedented technological progress.

The main differences between ML and AI are shown in Table 1.

Key Differences Between Machine Learning and Neural Networks

Aspect	Machine Learning	Neural Networks
Definition	Broad field that includes algorithms and models to make predictions or decisions based on data.	A subset of machine learning focused on algorithms inspired by the structure of the human brain.
Model Complexity	Includes simpler models like linear regression, decision trees, and SVMs.	Typically more complex, involving multiple interconnected layers (deep learning).
Data Requirements	Works well with small to medium-sized datasets.	Requires large datasets to perform effectively and avoid overfitting.

Table 1

AI's origins are not new; they trace back decades. Early AI included simple algorithms designed for games like chess or basic mathematical problems, which evolved into more sophisticated systems. These advanced systems can perform intricate tasks, such as the expert systems from the 1970s and 1980s. These systems, which employ rules and data to make decisions in specialized fields like medicine or engineering, demonstrated AI's practical applications.

The history of Artificial Intelligence (AI) began in the mid-20th century, when the term was first coined by computer scientist John McCarthy at the 1956 Dartmouth Conference. Early AI focused on symbolic processing, with pioneers like Alan Turing, who proposed the Turing Test as a measure of machine intelligence in 1950, and Marvin Minsky, who made foundational contributions to AI theory. The 1960s and 1970s saw limited progress due to hardware constraints and lack of data. However, by the 1980s, advances in machine learning and neural networks began to emerge, though funding and enthusiasm fluctuated due to what is often called the "AI winter."

The 1990s and 2000s brought renewed interest, with breakthroughs in statistical learning and algorithms capable of pattern recognition. By the 2010s, rapid developments in deep learning, driven by improved computational power and large data sets, led to transformative applications in natural language processing, vision, and decision-making systems. AI has since become deeply embedded in everyday technology, transforming industries, and sparking ongoing debates about its ethical and societal impacts.

CHAPTER SUMMARY DIAGRAM:

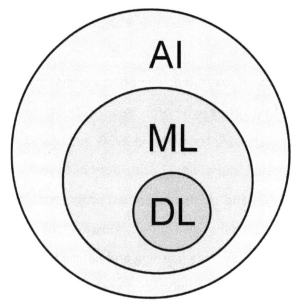

Figure 1: Relationship between AI, ML, and DL

Knowledge Check:

This exercise is to check if you understood the main points of this chapter. Assume you are an entrepreneur, and you are asked to use one of the approaches learnt above. This is just a short exercise to check the concepts.

EXERCISE: PREDICTING HOUSING PRICES

In this exercise, you will create a model to predict housing prices based on historical data. You will use a dataset containing information such as the number of rooms, square footage, location, and price of houses.

Objective: Build a model that predicts house prices and evaluate its performance.

What kind of model is the best approach to use?

    a. Neural Network

    b. Machine Learning

Can this model be built using both approaches?

    a. Yes

    b. No

REFERENCES:

- Aggarwal, C. C., & Zhai, C. (2012). A Survey of Text Clustering Algorithms. In Mining Text Data (pp. 77-128). Springer. Retrieved from https://link.springer.com/chapter/10.1007/978-1-4614-3223-4_4

- McCarthy, J. (2006). What is Artificial Intelligence?

- Russell, S., & Norvig, P. (2010). Artificial Intelligence: A Modern Approach.

- Turing, A. M. (1950). Computing Machinery and Intelligence. Mind, 59(236), 433–460.

- Xu, R., & Wunsch, D. (2005). Survey of clustering algorithms. IEEE Transactions on Neural Networks, 16(3), 645-678. Retrieved from https://ieeexplore.ieee.org/document/1427769

CHAPTER 2: TYPES OF AI

Artificial Intelligence (AI) isn't some singular, all-encompassing entity; it's more like a toolbox filled with specialized instruments, each crafted for a unique purpose. Understanding the various types of AI is not just an academic exercise—it's the key to appreciating its potential and recognizing its limitations. Let's explore the main categories: Narrow AI vs. General AI, Weak AI vs. Strong AI, and the fascinating, if speculative, idea of Superintelligence. We'll also dive into specialized types like generative AI, expert systems, inference engines, reasoning engines, and more.

Inference and Reasoning Engines vs. Large Language Models (LLMs)

AI can be broadly categorized into systems that rely on predefined rules for decision-making and those that generate responses based on learned patterns. Two key categories in this distinction are inference/reasoning engines and large language models (LLMs).

INFERENCE/REASONING ENGINES: LOGIC-BASED AI

Inference engines, sometimes called reasoning engines, operate based on explicit rules and logic. These systems rely on structured data, using a set of predefined rules (if-then statements) to draw conclusions. They are widely used in expert systems where precise decision-making is required, such as:

- **Medical diagnosis**: AI models that assess symptoms and match them to potential diseases based on a database of medical knowledge.
- **Financial risk assessment**: Systems that analyze financial transactions for fraud detection.
- **Legal decision-making**: AI that applies legal principles to provide guidance based on case law.

These engines do not "learn" from new data unless manually updated. Their strength is in their reliability and explainability, but they lack the flexibility to adapt beyond their programmed knowledge.

LARGE LANGUAGE MODELS (LLMS): PATTERN-BASED AI

LLMs, like ChatGPT and Google Gemini, are trained on massive datasets and use probability-based predictions to generate human-like responses. They recognize patterns in language and generate text based on context rather than strict logic.

- **Chatbots and Virtual Assistants**: LLMs power conversational agents that respond fluidly to user input.
- **Content Generation**: These models can create articles, scripts, and even poetry based on learned patterns.
- **Customer Support Automation**: LLMs handle inquiries by predicting the best responses based on past interactions.

Unlike inference engines, LLMs do not operate on strict logical deductions but instead generate responses based on the probability of word sequences from their training

27

data. This makes them highly flexible but also prone to inaccuracies (hallucinations).

HOW LLMS WORK (LIKE A SMART GUESSING GAME!)

Imagine you have a giant book that has all the sentences ever written in it. Every time you start a sentence, the book helps you guess what comes next.

For example, if you say "Once upon a...", the book will tell you that the next word is "time" because that's what usually comes next.

This is how Large Language Models (LLMs) work! Instead of a book, they use lots and lots of examples from the internet to guess what comes next in a sentence.

But here's the thing—they don't actually understand what they're saying. They're just really good at guessing what sounds right!

It's like playing a game where you try to finish someone else's sentence based on what makes sense. Sometimes, they get it perfect, and sometimes, they guess a little weirdly because they don't actually "think" like humans do.

GENERATIVE AI: THE CREATIVE THINKERS

Generative AI is like an artist with an infinite palette, capable of producing text, images, music, and videos by recognizing and replicating patterns from massive datasets. Instead of merely analyzing and interpreting information like traditional AI, generative AI creates something entirely new—like a builder with a limitless box of LEGO bricks, each piece representing data and learned knowledge. Just as those LEGO blocks can be assembled in infinite ways to form castles, spaceships, or entirely new designs, generative AI constructs original content based on its understanding of relationships and structures within the data it has encountered.

HOW IT WORKS: MORE THAN JUST GUESSING

At first glance, generative AI might seem like it's simply guessing what should come next, much like how a child completing the phrase "Once upon a..." instinctively adds "time." But the real magic lies in how it refines those predictions. By studying millions of examples, it learns the nuances of storytelling, the structure of a painting, or the harmonies of a song, allowing it to produce results that are both innovative and contextually relevant. This is where techniques like Generative Adversarial Networks (GANs) and Variational Autoencoders (VAEs) come into play, ensuring that AI doesn't just regurgitate what it has seen but instead generates something fresh, unique, and valuable.

THE DIFFERENCE BETWEEN GENERATIVE AI AND OTHER AI

While expert systems and inference engines rely on strict, predefined rules, and large language models (LLMs) generate text based on probability, generative AI moves into the realm of open-ended creation. Traditional AI finds the best answer from existing data, whereas generative AI produces new possibilities. It's the difference between asking a recipe chatbot for a cake recipe and asking it to invent an entirely new type of dessert.

Key Differences Between Inference/Reasoning Engines and LLMs

Feature	Inference/Reasoning Engine	Large Language Model (LLM)
Core Function	Deductive reasoning using rules	Pattern recognition & text prediction
Data Source	Explicit rules & facts	Large-scale training data (text)
Type of Output	Logical conclusions	Probabilistic language generation
Flexibility	Rigid, needs manual updates	Adaptive, but can hallucinate (make stuff up)
Example Use	Diagnosing diseases, legal decision-making	Chatbots, creative writing, customer service

HOW THEY WORK TOGETHER

Some advanced AI systems combine both approaches. For example, an LLM might generate possible answers, while an inference engine verifies their accuracy before presenting the final response. This hybrid approach is increasingly used in industries where accuracy and adaptability are both required.

Relationship Between Inference Engines, LLMs, and Narrow vs. General AI

Both inference engines and LLMs fall under **Narrow AI**, as they are specialized tools designed to perform specific tasks within a limited scope.

- **Inference/Reasoning Engines** belong to the category of **expert systems**, a subset of Narrow AI that follows predefined rules and logic for decision-making.
- **LLMs** also fit into Narrow AI but take a different approach, using probability and pattern recognition rather than strict logical reasoning.

CONNECTION TO GENERAL AI

General AI (AGI) would be an **entirely different category** from either inference engines or LLMs. While these systems are excellent at their predefined tasks, **AGI would be capable of adapting, reasoning, and learning across multiple domains**—much like a human. Neither inference engines nor LLMs currently possess this level of adaptability or understanding.

Thus, inference engines provide structured, logic-driven AI, while LLMs bring flexibility and pattern-based learning. Both serve different purposes but remain limited compared to the broader, adaptable intelligence of AGI.

Narrow AI vs. General AI

NARROW AI: MASTERS OF ONE

Narrow AI, also known as Artificial Narrow Intelligence (ANI), is like the champion specialist in a specific field. It's what powers Netflix's eerily accurate recommendations, your phone's voice assistants, and the systems scanning millions of transactions to detect fraud. Narrow AI shines because it's laser-focused. These systems are trained on specific datasets to solve specific problems.

Take these examples:

- **Healthcare**: AI models like IBM Watson analyze mountains of medical data to assist in diagnosis.
- **Finance**: Fraud detection systems flag unusual activity in your accounts.
- **Retail**: Recommendation engines tailor shopping experiences to individual preferences.

However, Narrow AI can't go beyond its training. Ask it to step outside its lane—say, to switch from recommending movies to designing supply chain logistics—and it's as lost as a GPS with no signal.

GENERAL AI: THE GREAT DREAM

General AI, or Artificial General Intelligence (AGI), is the elusive concept of machines that can think, reason, and learn like humans. Imagine a system that could adapt to any situation, solve new problems, and maybe even debate complex philosophical questions.

With the release of OpenAI's GPT-4.5 and o3 models in 2025, we are inching closer to AGI. These models demonstrate remarkable capabilities in understanding and generating human-like language, performing multi-modal tasks, and learning from limited input. However, they remain specialized tools rather than truly general systems. Bridging the gap to AGI will require breakthroughs in cognitive flexibility, contextual understanding, and integration of knowledge across domains.

Weak AI vs. Strong AI

WEAK AI: USEFUL BUT LIMITED

Weak AI is a misnomer. It's not weak in performance but limited in scope. These systems simulate intelligence by following predefined rules and processing data efficiently, but they're not conscious or self-aware.

Here are some examples:

- Chatbots that answer customer questions with natural language processing.
- Autonomous vehicles navigating roads by analyzing sensor data.
- Medical imaging tools identifying tumors in X-rays or MRIs.

Weak AI is a tool—powerful within its designed purpose but utterly dependent on human direction. It doesn't "think" like you or me; it just processes inputs and spits out outputs.

STRONG AI: MACHINES WITH MINDS

Strong AI, or Artificial Strong Intelligence (ASI), is a theoretical concept of machines that possess self-awareness, genuine understanding, and emotions. This level of AI would cross the boundary from tool to being.

Achieving Strong AI would require solving some of the biggest mysteries of existence:

- **What is consciousness?** Could it be replicated in a machine?
- **What are the ethical implications?** Would a sentient machine deserve rights?

No one has built a Strong AI yet, but the concept continues to challenge how we think about intelligence, ethics, and humanity.

Specialized Types of AI

AI has evolved into various specialized categories, each tailored for unique applications and capabilities. Here are some of the most significant ones:

GENERATIVE AI: THE CREATIVE THINKERS

Generative AI systems create new content—whether text, images, audio, or video—based on patterns learned from existing data. Tools like GPT (for text generation), DALL-E (for image creation), and others have transformed industries. Examples include:

- **ChatGPT** by OpenAI: A conversational AI that generates human-like text for various applications.
- **Claude** by Anthropic: A model designed for insightful, ethical, and reliable AI interactions.
- **Google Gemini**: A multi-modal AI model that integrates text, images, and more for creative and analytical tasks.

Generative AI has found applications in writing, design, entertainment, and even product development, revolutionizing creative industries.

EXPERT SYSTEMS: THE KNOWLEDGE ENGINES

Expert systems emulate decision-making abilities of human experts. These systems rely on a set of predefined rules and a database of facts to solve complex problems. For example:

- **Medical Diagnosis**: Systems that assist doctors by providing possible diagnoses based on symptoms.
- **Engineering**: Tools that recommend optimal solutions for intricate design problems.

REINFORCEMENT LEARNING: THE TRIAL-AND-ERROR LEARNERS

Reinforcement learning involves training AI through a system of rewards and penalties. It's particularly effective in dynamic environments, such as:

- **Gaming**: AI agents mastering complex games like Go or StarCraft.
- **Robotics**: Robots learning to navigate spaces or perform tasks autonomously.

EVOLUTIONARY AI: ADAPTING THROUGH ITERATION

Inspired by biological evolution, evolutionary AI optimizes solutions over generations by simulating natural selection. This approach is widely used in optimization problems, like designing efficient networks or scheduling systems.

HYBRID AI: THE BEST OF ALL WORLDS

Hybrid AI combines multiple AI types to create systems that are more versatile and effective. For example, a hybrid model might use natural language processing (NLP) for understanding human input and reinforcement learning for decision-making.

Superintelligence: A Thought Experiment

WHAT IS SUPERINTELLIGENCE?

Superintelligence, as philosopher Nick Bostrom describes it, is an AI that surpasses human intelligence in every conceivable way. Think of an entity that's not only faster at calculations but also more creative, insightful, and socially adept than the best of us.

WHY SOME BELIEVE IT'S POSSIBLE

If AGI is achieved, it might be capable of self-improvement—a feedback loop leading to exponential growth in intelligence, often called an "intelligence explosion."

Critics point out several roadblocks:

- **Resources**: The computational and energy demands could be insurmountable.
- **Control**: How do we ensure a superintelligent AI aligns with human values?
- **Speculation**: Without evidence, superintelligence remains a provocative idea rather than a practical concern.

Whether you see superintelligence as inevitable or improbable, its potential implications are too significant to ignore.

Key Takeaways

- Narrow AI dominates today, excelling at specific tasks but lacking adaptability.
- General AI remains a distant dream, promising systems that think and learn like humans.
- Weak AI is practical and widespread, while Strong AI raises profound ethical and philosophical questions.
- Inference engines follow strict logic and rules, while LLMs rely on pattern recognition and probability.
- Generative AI and expert systems are transforming industries through creativity and specialized decision-making.
- Models like ChatGPT, Claude, and Google Gemini highlight generative AI's real-world impact.

- Superintelligence captivates futurists but remains a speculative frontier.

As AI continues to evolve, understanding these distinctions helps us prepare for the opportunities and challenges ahead. Each type represents a step forward, reshaping industries, societies, and our understanding of intelligence itself.

Knowledge Check

This exercise is to ensure you understood the main points from this chapter. Assume you are explaining AI types to a non-technical business leader and are asked to recommend suitable applications. This is a short conceptual exercise; for detailed implementations or examples, you may consult additional resources.

Questions:

1. What is the primary difference between Narrow AI and General AI?
   a. Narrow AI is task-specific, while General AI adapts to various tasks.
   b. Narrow AI requires more computational power than General AI.
   c. General AI is already widely implemented in industries today.
   d. Narrow AI and General AI are fundamentally the same.
2. Which type of AI simulates intelligence without being self-aware?
   a. Strong AI
   b. Weak AI

c. Generative A
d. Superintelligence
3. Can generative AI be used in industries beyond writing and design?
   a. Yes
   b. No
4. True or False: Reinforcement learning uses predefined rules to solve problems.
5. Describe one ethical challenge associated with Strong AI.

EXERCISE: RECOMMENDING AI APPLICATIONS

Scenario:
You are consulting for a healthcare organization that wants to leverage AI for both administrative efficiency and patient care. Based on this chapter, suggest which type of AI fits the following needs:

1. **Administrative Task Automation:** Scheduling, billing, and resource allocation.
2. **Patient Diagnosis Assistance:** Analyzing medical images for tumors.
3. **Exploratory Research:** Developing new treatment protocols using iterative learning models.

Objective: Clearly justify your choice of Narrow AI, Generative AI, Expert Systems, or Reinforcement Learning for each scenario.

- OpenAI. (2025). *GPT-4.5 and o3 Models Documentation*. OpenAI Research.
- Bostrom, N. (2014). *Superintelligence: Paths, Dangers, Strategies*. Oxford University Press.
- IBM Watson. (n.d.). *Healthcare AI Solutions*. Retrieved from IBM Watson.
- Anthropic. (n.d.). *Claude: Ethical AI Systems for Safer Interactions*. Retrieved from Anthropic.
- Google. (n.d.). *Google Gemini AI Model Overview*. Retrieved from Google AI.
- McCarthy, J. (2006). *What is Artificial Intelligence?*. Stanford University.

This list reflects the chapter's references to specific tools (like IBM Watson, Claude, and Google Gemini), as well as notable AI literature and advancements.

CHAPTER 3:
DEEP LEARNING AND NEURAL NETWORKS

BASIC CONCEPTS:
WHY IS IT CALLED DEEP LEARNING?

Neural Networks are designed to mimic human brain cells called neurons. Deep Learning gets its name from the multiple layers of neurons in neural networks, which allow the model to learn and represent data in increasingly complex ways. Each layer, or "depth," processes the input data to a higher level of abstraction. For example, in image recognition, the initial layers might identify simple features like edges, while deeper layers recognize more complex patterns and objects. This hierarchical structure enables the network to make sense of intricate data and deliver highly accurate predictions and insights. The term "deep" emphasizes the depth of these layers, which differentiates it from traditional machine learning approaches. The more layers, the "deeper" the network, and the more capable it becomes at handling sophisticated tasks.

Brain learns by observation through eyes and sending signals to the brain which adjust what we call weights until learning happens. A neuron, often referred to as a nerve cell, is the fundamental building block of the nervous system. Neurons are specialized cells responsible for transmitting information throughout the body using electrical and chemical signals. This process involves the neuron receiving inputs through its dendrites, processing the information in the cell body, and then sending signals out through its axon to other neurons or to muscles and glands. These signals help the brain to process sensory information, control motor functions, and facilitate cognitive processes such as learning and memory. By adjusting the strength or 'weights' of the connections between neurons, the brain can learn from experiences and adapt over time, continually refining its responses based on new information. This dynamic capability of neurons to change and strengthen connections or weights, is a key component of how learning and memory occur in the brain.

Typically, the input enters through our visual senses and as learning happens, the outputs are recognized. This process involves the brain decoding visual stimuli received through the eyes and transmitting these signals to the visual cortex. As we interact with our environment, the brain continuously adjusts its neural connections based on the feedback it receives, a phenomenon known as synaptic plasticity. This constant reconfiguration allows for the refinement of skills and the enhancement of our ability to recognize patterns and objects. Over time, with repeated exposure and practice, these neural pathways strengthen, leading to more accurate and faster recognition of the outputs, such as identifying faces, reading, or navigating complex environments. This dynamic interplay between input and output is fundamental to learning and memory formation. A simple Neural Network is shown in figure 2.

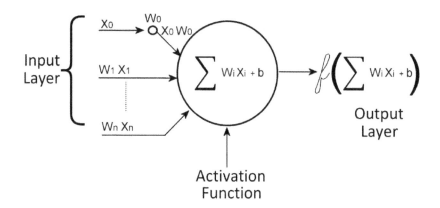

FIGURE 2 (A SIMPLE NEURAL NETWORK)

ARCHITECTURES OF NEURAL NETWORKS

A NN can be implemented using many architectures. Some

of the most common algorithms used in neural networks

are as follows:

1. **Backpropagation**: This algorithm is fundamental
   for training neural networks. It involves adjusting
   the weights of the neurons by propagating the
   error backward from the output layer to the input
   layer. Backpropagation is a fundamental algorithm
   used to train artificial neural networks. It is short
   for "backward propagation of errors" and involves
   adjusting the weights of the neurons in a network
   to minimize the error in the output.

2. **Stochastic Gradient Descent (SGD)**: This optimization algorithm is used to minimize the loss function by updating the weights incrementally, one training example at a time, which makes it more efficient for large datasets.

3. **Adam (Adaptive Moment Estimation)**: An extension of SGD, Adam computes adaptive learning rates for each parameter. It combines the advantages of two other extensions of SGD, namely, RMSProp and AdaGrad.

4. **Convolutional Neural Networks (CNNs)**: These are specialized neural networks primarily used for image and video recognition. They use convolutional layers to automatically and adaptively learn spatial hierarchies of features.

5. **Recurrent Neural Networks (RNNs)**: Particularly useful for sequential data, RNNs maintain a memory of previous inputs, making them suitable for tasks such as language modeling and time series prediction.

6. **Long Short-Term Memory Networks (LSTMs)**: A type of RNN that can learn long-term dependencies, addressing the vanishing gradient problem common in standard RNNs.

7. **Autoencoders**: These unsupervised learning models are used for tasks like dimensionality reduction and feature learning. They work by encoding the input into a compressed representation and then reconstructing the input from this representation.

8. **Generative Adversarial Networks (GANs)**: Comprising two networks, a generator and a discriminator, GANs are used to generate new data samples that mimic a given distribution, commonly used in image generation and synthesis.

9. **Restricted Boltzmann Machines (RBMs)**: These are stochastic neural networks that can learn a probability distribution over its set of inputs. They are used in recommendation systems and feature learning.

10. **Transformer Networks**: These networks have revolutionized natural language processing by using mechanisms like self-attention to handle long-range dependencies more efficiently. They are the backbone of many state-of-the-art language models.

These algorithms and models are essential in a wide range of applications, from image and speech recognition to natural language processing and beyond.

Top 3 most-used algorithms:

Here are the top three most-used algorithms based on their impact and frequency of use in modern machine learning and AI applications:

1. Convolutional Neural Networks (CNNs)

Example:

CNNs are widely used in image recognition tasks. For instance, a CNN can identify objects in photographs, such as cats or dogs, by applying convolutional filters to detect features like edges, textures, and shapes. For example, in the ImageNet Classification Challenge, CNNs revolutionized performance, with architectures like

AlexNet achieving remarkable accuracy by learning hierarchical visual patterns.

2. Stochastic Gradient Descent (SGD)

Example:

SGD is fundamental in training neural networks by optimizing weights iteratively. For example, during training a logistic regression model for spam detection, SGD updates the model parameters using one email (or a small batch of emails) at a time rather than the entire dataset. This approach significantly speeds up training, particularly for large datasets, while approximating the gradient effectively.

3. Transformer Networks

Example:

Transformers are the backbone of modern Natural Language Processing (NLP). For example, models like GPT (Generative Pre-trained Transformer) generate coherent and contextually appropriate text for tasks like essay writing or chatbot interactions. They use mechanisms like self-attention to understand the relationships between words in a sentence without relying on sequence order.

Each of these algorithms has revolutionized its domain, making them indispensable tools in machine learning.

Structure of a Neural Network

A neural network consists of an input layer, one or more hidden layers, and an output layer. Each layer is composed of nodes, also known as neurons. The connections between these nodes have associated weights, which are adjusted during the training process. These adjustments help the brain with the learning process.

FORWARD PASS
The forward pass is the process of the input data going through the input layer, hidden layers, and output layer.

1. **Input Layer**: The input data is fed into the network through the input layer.

2. **Hidden Layers**: The data passes through each hidden layer. Neurons in these layers apply a weighted sum of the inputs plus a bias, and then an activation function (like ReLU or sigmoid) is applied to introduce non-linearity. The bias is applied to reduce overfitting.

3. **Output Layer**: The final layer produces the network's output, which is compared to the desired output to compute the error.

BACKWARD PASS (BACKPROPAGATION)

The goal of backpropagation is to reduce the error by adjusting the weights. This process involves the following steps:

1. **Calculate Error**: Compute the error at the output layer using a loss function (e.g., Mean Squared Error for regression tasks or Cross-Entropy Loss for classification tasks).

2. **Backpropagate Error**: The error is propagated backwards through the network. This involves:

   - **Output Layer**: Calculate the gradient of the loss function with respect to the output, and then use this gradient to compute the error for the weights in the output layer.

   - **Hidden Layers**: For each layer, the error is further propagated back, calculating the gradient of the loss function with respect to the output of that layer. This involves using the chain rule to calculate the gradient of the loss with respect to the weights in each layer. In a neural network using the backpropagation algorithm, the error is propagated back and distributed to different inputs, but in a structured way based on the network's weights, activations, and structure.

3. **Update Weights**: Adjust the weights using the calculated gradients. This is typically done using an optimization algorithm like Stochastic Gradient Descent (SGD) or Adam. The weights are updated to reduce the loss:

ITERATIVE PROCESS

The forward and backward passes are repeated iteratively over many iterations called epochs, with the data being fed through the network multiple times. During each iteration, the weights are adjusted to minimize the error further. This iterative process allows the neural network to learn patterns in the data and make accurate predictions.

Activation functions like ReLU (Rectified Linear Unit), sigmoid, or tanh introduce non-linearity into the network, allowing it to learn complex patterns. Without activation functions, the neural network would be limited to learning only linear or much easier relationships. For a good understanding of an activation function, mathematics, data, and programming are essential tools.

Challenges and Considerations

- **Vanishing Gradients**: In deep networks, gradients can become very small, slowing down learning. Techniques like gradient clipping or advanced activation functions like ReLU help mitigate this issue.

- **Overfitting**: If the network is too complex, it might perform well on training data but poorly on unseen data. Regularization techniques like dropout or L2 regularization help prevent overfitting. The introduction of bias also reduces overfitting.

- **Learning Rate**: Choosing the right learning rate is crucial. A rate that is too high can cause the network to converge too quickly to a suboptimal solution, while a rate that is too low can make training very slow.

Backpropagation is powerful, and when combined with other techniques and optimizations, it forms the foundation of modern deep learning.

RECENT BREAKTHROUGHS AND APPLICATIONS

Some of the recent breakthroughs and applications in deep learning are as follows:

1. **Graph Neural Networks (GNNs)**: GNNs have shown great promise in understanding and leveraging relationships within data. They are particularly useful in social network analysis, recommendation systems, and predicting the properties of new materials (Xu et al., 2019; Kipf & Welling, 2017).

2. **Generative Adversarial Networks (GANs)**: GANs have advanced significantly, enabling the creation of highly realistic images, videos, and even music. Applications range from art generation to improving the realism of synthetic data for training other models (Goodfellow et al., 2014; Karras et al., 2020).

3. **Transformers**: Originally developed for natural language processing, transformers have revolutionized the field with models like Chat GPT-3 and BERT. They are now being adapted for tasks in computer vision, protein folding, and more (Vaswani et al., 2017; Brown et al., 2020).

4. **Self-Supervised Learning**: This approach, where models learn to understand data by predicting parts of it, has led to significant improvements in unsupervised learning tasks, reducing the need for labeled data (Chen et al., 2020; He et al., 2020).

5. **Neural Architecture Search (NAS)**: NAS automates the process of designing neural network architectures, leading to the discovery of more efficient and effective models (Zoph & Le, 2017; Real et al., 2019).

6. **Explainable AI (XAI)**: There is a growing focus on making deep learning models more interpretable and transparent, crucial for applications in healthcare, finance, and other areas (Ribeiro et al., 2016; Doshi-Velez & Kim, 2017).

Applications of Deep Learning

1. **Healthcare**: Deep learning is used for medical image analysis, predicting patient outcomes, and even drug discovery (Esteva et al., 2017; Topol, 2019).

2. **Autonomous Vehicles**: Self-driving cars rely on deep learning for tasks like object detection, path planning, and decision making (Bojarski et al., 2016; Chen et al., 2015).

3. **Natural Language Processing (NLP)**: Applications include language translation, sentiment analysis, and chatbots (Devlin et al., 2018; Radford et al., 2019).

4. **Finance**: Fraud detection, algorithmic trading, and risk management are areas where deep learning is making a significant impact (Heaton et al., 2016; Sirignano & Cont, 2019).

5. **Entertainment**: Deep learning is used in content recommendation systems, game development, and even creating realistic special effects (Covington et al., 2016; Liang et al., 2018).

6. **Agriculture**: Precision farming techniques use deep learning for crop monitoring, yield prediction, and pest detection (Kamilaris & Prenafeta-Boldú, 2018; Chlingaryan et al., 2018).

CHAPTER 3 SUMMARY TABLE:

Architectures:
Backpropagation, Stochastic Gradient Descent (SGD), Adam (Adaptive Moment Estimation), Convolutional Neural Networks (CNNs), Recurrent Neural Networks (RNNs), Long Short-Term Memory Networks (LSTMs), Autoencoders, Generative Adversarial Networks (GANs), Restricted Boltzmann Machines (RBMs), Transformer Networks
Applications:
Healthcare, Autonomous Vehicles, Natural Language Processing, Finance, Entertainment, Agriculture

Knowledge Check:

This exercise is to check if you understood the main points of this chapter. Assume you are an entrepreneur, and you are asked to use one of the approaches learnt above. This is just a short exercise to check the concepts.

EXERCISE: PREDICTING HOUSE PRICES

You are provided with a dataset containing information about houses and their respective prices. The goal is to build a predictive model using a Neural Network to minimize the mean squared error (MSE) between predicted and actual house prices. The training of a deep network is needed to accurately map input features to output targets by adjusting weights efficiently.

Which architecture would you recommend?

    a. Backpropagation

    b. Stochastic Gradient Descent

    c. Convolutional Neural Network

    d. Recurrent Neural Network

Exercise: Diagnosing Skin Cancer from Dermatoscopic Images

You need to train a Neural Network to classify dermatoscopic images of skin lesions into categories such as benign or malignant. The dataset contains thousands of high-resolution images with pixel-level detail to extract spatial hierarchies of features. Starting with basic edge detection in the early layers, the network can progressively learn complex patterns like texture, shape, and color variations associated with cancerous lesions.

Which architecture will you use?

a. Backpropagation
b. Stochastic Gradient Descent
c. Adam (Adaptive Moment Estimation)
d. Convolutional Neural Networks

Exercise: Training a Logistic Regression Model on a Massive Streaming Dataset

In this exercise, you are tasked with building a logistic regression model to classify user clicks in a real-time advertisement system. The dataset is vast and continuously streaming, making it impractical to load the entire data into memory or perform batch processing.

Which architecture will you use?

e. Backpropagation
f. Stochastic Gradient Descent

g. Adam (Adaptive Moment Estimation)

h. Convolutional Neural Networks

Exercise: Translating Scientific Papers Between Languages

In this exercise, you are tasked with developing a machine translation system to translate scientific papers from English to French while preserving context and technical accuracy. Unlike traditional sequence-based models like RNNs or LSTMs, we need an architecture that can process entire sequences simultaneously, capturing long-range dependencies and relationships across sentences. This capability is critical for understanding complex sentences and technical terminology typical of scientific papers. Other models, which struggle with lengthy contexts or lose track of dependencies, would fail to provide the high-quality translations required for this task.

Which architecture will you use?

i. Backpropagation

j. Stochastic Gradient Descent

K. Transformer Neural Network

l. Convolutional Neural Networks

CITATIONS:

- Brown, T. B., Mann, B., Ryder, N., Subbiah, M., Kaplan, J. D., Dhariwal, P., ... & Amodei, D. (2020). Language models are few-shot learners. Advances in neural information processing systems, 33, 1877-1901.

- Bottou, L. (2010). Large-scale machine learning with stochastic gradient descent. In *Proceedings of COMPSTAT* (pp. 177-186). Springer.

- Chen, T., Kornblith, S., Norouzi, M., & Hinton, G. (2020). A simple framework for contrastive learning of visual representations. In International conference on machine learning (pp. 1597-1607). PMLR.

- Chen, X., Ma, H., Wan, J., Li, B., & Xia, T. (2015). Multi-view 3d object detection network for autonomous driving. In Proceedings of the IEEE conference on computer vision and pattern recognition (pp. 1907-1915).

- Chlingaryan, A., Sukkarieh, S., & Whelan, B. (2018). Machine learning approaches for crop yield prediction and nitrogen status estimation in precision agriculture: A review. Computers and electronics in agriculture, 151, 61-69.

- Covington, P., Adams, J., & Sargin, E. (2016, September). Deep neural networks for YouTube recommendations. In Proceedings of the 10th ACM conference on recommender systems (pp. 191-198).

- Devlin, J., Chang, M. W., Lee, K., & Toutanova, K. (2018). Bert: Pre-training of deep bidirectional transformers for language understanding. arXiv preprint arXiv:1810.04805.

- Doshi-Velez, F., & Kim, B. (2017). Towards a rigorous science of interpretable machine learning. arXiv preprint arXiv:1702.08608.

- Esteva, A., Kuprel, B., Novoa, R. A., Ko, J., Swetter, S. M., Blau, H. M., & Thrun, S. (2017).

Dermatologist-level classification of skin cancer with deep neural networks. Nature, 542(7639), 115-118.

- Goodfellow, I., Pouget-Abadie, J., Mirza, M., Xu, B., Warde-Farley, D., Ozair, S., ... & Bengio, Y. (2014). Generative adversarial nets. Advances in neural information processing systems, 27.

- He, K., Fan, H., Wu, Y., Xie, S., & Girshick, R. (2020). Momentum contrast for unsupervised visual representation learning. In Proceedings of the IEEE/CVF conference on computer vision and pattern recognition (pp. 9729-9738).

- Heaton, J. B., Polson, N. G., & Witte, J. H. (2016). Deep learning in finance. arXiv preprint arXiv:1602.06561.

- Kamilaris, A., & Prenafeta-Boldú, F. X. (2018). Deep learning in agriculture: A survey. Computers and electronics in agriculture, 147, 70-90.

- Karras, T., Laine, S., & Aila, T. (2020). A style-based generator architecture for generative adversarial networks. IEEE transactions on pattern analysis and machine intelligence, 41(12), 3170-3180.

- Kipf, T. N., & Welling, M. (2017). Semi-supervised classification with graph convolutional networks. arXiv preprint arXiv:1609.02907.

- LeCun, Y., Bengio, Y., & Hinton, G. (2015). Deep learning. *Nature*, 521(7553), 436-444.

- Liang, D., Krishnan, R. G., Hoffman, M. D., & Jebara, T. (2018). Variational autoencoders for collaborative filtering. In Proceedings of the 2018 world wide web conference (pp. 689-698).

- Radford, A., Wu, J., Amodei, D., Amodei, D., Clark, J., Brundage, M., ... & Sutskever, I. (2019). Language models are unsupervised multitask learners. OpenAI blog, 1(8), 9.

- Real, E., Aggarwal, A., Huang, Y., & Le, Q. V. (2019). Regularized evolution for image classifier architecture search. In Proceedings of the aaai conference on artificial intelligence (Vol. 33, pp. 4780-4789).

- Ribeiro, M. T., Singh, S., & Guestrin, C. (2016, August). "Why should I trust you?" Explaining the predictions of any classifier. In Proceedings of the 22nd ACM SIGKDD international conference on knowledge discovery and data mining (pp. 1135-1144).

- Sirignano, J., & Cont, R. (2019). Universal features of price formation in financial markets: perspectives from deep learning. Quantitative Finance, 19(9), 1449-1459.

- Topol, E. J. (2019). High-performance medicine: the convergence of human and artificial intelligence. Nature medicine, 25(1), 44-56.

- Vaswani, A., Shazeer, N., Parmar, N., Uszkoreit, J., Jones, L., Gomez, A. N., ... & Polosukhin, I. (2017). Attention is all you need. Advances in neural information processing systems, 30.

- Xu, K., Hu, W., Leskovec, J., & Jegelka, S. (2019). How powerful are graph neural networks? arXiv preprint arXiv:1810.00826.

- Zoph, B., & Le, Q. V. (2017). Neural architecture search with reinforcement learning. arXiv preprint arXiv:1611.01578.

Artificial Intelligence (AI) isn't just a concept for sci-fi films or tech-savvy professionals anymore. It's quietly embedded in our daily lives, often operating in the background, making things easier, faster, and more efficient. From the moment we wake up to the time we go to bed, AI is there—whether it's helping us navigate morning traffic, recommending a new TV show, or keeping our homes comfortable and secure. In this chapter, we'll explore the everyday presence of AI, shedding light on its role across industries and the transformative impact it's had on our routines.

AI Everywhere: Industry Spotlights

AI has proven to be a game-changer across multiple sectors. Let's take a closer look at a few industries where AI has truly made its mark:

HEALTHCARE

Imagine your doctor having a superpower—that's AI in healthcare.

- **Medical Imaging:** AI tools analyze X-rays, MRIs, and CT scans with precision, often detecting diseases like cancer earlier and more accurately than human eyes can.
- **Predictive Analytics:** Hospitals now use AI to forecast patient needs, optimize staffing, and improve resource allocation.

- **Personalized Medicine:** Treatments tailored to your unique genetic makeup? AI makes that a reality, improving outcomes and reducing side effects.

FINANCE

AI acts as both the brains and the bouncer in financial systems.

- **Fraud Detection:** Algorithms spot suspicious activity faster than you can say "identity theft."
- **Algorithmic Trading:** Split-second decisions in stock markets? That's AI at work, capitalizing on trends before humans can react.
- **Credit Scoring:** AI expands access to credit by evaluating factors beyond traditional credit scores.

RETAIL AND E-COMMERCE

Your shopping experience, online or in-store, owes a lot to AI.

- **Recommendation Engines:** Platforms like Amazon and Netflix tailor suggestions to your preferences, almost like they know you better than your best friend.
- **Virtual Assistants:** Chatbots handle customer inquiries at any hour, resolving issues in record time.
- **Inventory Management:** AI forecasts demand, ensuring stores don't run out of what you need.

Getting from point A to B has never been smoother.

- **Route Optimization:** Apps like Google Maps use real-time data to guide you through traffic jams and roadblocks.
- **Self-Driving Cars:** AI-powered vehicles from companies like Tesla are paving the way for safer, autonomous commutes.
- **Fleet Management:** Logistics firms use AI to track vehicle health and streamline deliveries.

ENTERTAINMENT

Whether you're binge-watching or gaming, AI is your behind-the-scenes producer.

- **Content Curation:** Streaming platforms recommend shows and playlists tailored to your tastes.
- **Gaming:** AI opponents learn your strategies, making games more engaging.
- **Creative Tools:** AI is even helping musicians and artists create, blending human ingenuity with machine precision.

AI for Consumers: Making Life Smarter

AI's impact isn't confined to industries; it's right in your living room (and pocket) too. Here's how AI has become a part of everyday life:

Siri, Alexa, and Google Assistant have become household names, performing tasks like:

- Answering questions
- Setting reminders
- Controlling smart home gadgets
- Delivering weather updates These virtual helpers use natural language processing to continually improve their conversational skills, becoming more intuitive with every interaction.

SMART HOMES

Thanks to AI and the Internet of Things (IoT), homes are smarter than ever:

- **Thermostats:** Devices like Nest learn your schedule and preferences to optimize energy use.
- **Lighting:** Smart bulbs adjust to your routines and moods.
- **Security Systems:** AI-powered cameras and doorbells recognize faces and detect unusual activity.

WEARABLE TECH

Wearables like fitness trackers and smartwatches use AI to keep tabs on your health:

- **Activity Monitoring:** Track steps, calories burned, and sleep quality with personalized insights.

- **Health Alerts:** Devices monitor chronic conditions and alert you or your doctor when something's off.

The Invisible Hand of AI

Some of AI's most influential contributions work quietly in the background:

SOCIAL MEDIA ALGORITHMS

Ever wonder why your feed is so addictive? AI curates posts, ads, and content based on your behavior. While it keeps you scrolling, it's also sparked debates about privacy and echo chambers.

SEARCH ENGINES

AI ensures search results are fast and relevant. Tools like Google even predict what you're looking for before you finish typing.

EMAIL AND COMMUNICATION

AI helps declutter your inbox by filtering spam and suggesting replies, saving time and effort.

The Double-Edged Sword of AI

While AI's benefits are undeniable, it's not without challenges:

- **Convenience:** Automating repetitive tasks lets us focus on what matters.
- **Personalization:** From tailored ads to curated playlists, AI makes experiences feel custom-made.
- **Efficiency:** AI minimizes errors and maximizes productivity.

CHALLENGES

- **Privacy Issues:** AI relies on vast amounts of personal data, raising questions about security.
- **Dependence:** As we lean more on AI, there's a risk of losing critical thinking skills.
- **Bias:** AI can inherit biases from its training data, sometimes leading to unfair outcomes.

Wrapping Up

AI has woven itself into the fabric of daily life, reshaping industries and personal experiences alike. As we embrace its potential, it's equally important to navigate its challenges responsibly. By understanding how AI works and its implications, we can make better decisions—both as consumers and as contributors to a rapidly evolving world. Let's keep asking questions and pushing boundaries, ensuring that AI serves us all effectively and ethically.

Knowledge Check

This section checks your understanding of how AI impacts everyday life and industries. Assume you are a consultant explaining AI's applications to a small business owner.

Questions:

1. What is one way AI contributes to healthcare?
   a. By replacing doctors in surgeries
   b. Through personalized medicine and predictive analytics
   c. Creating general health awareness campaigns
   d. Designing hospital interiors
2. Which of these is NOT a feature of AI in transportation?
   a. Route optimization
   b. Fleet management
   c. Content curation
   d. Self-driving cars
3. True or False: AI-powered smart home devices like Nest thermostats learn your schedule and preferences to optimize energy use.
4. How does AI improve customer experience in retail?
   a. By automating store cleaning
   b. Through recommendation engines and chatbots
   c. By eliminating the need for sales associates
   d. By monitoring customer spending habits for banks
5. Describe one potential challenge of relying on AI in everyday life.

Scenario:
A local retail chain wants to adopt AI to improve its operations and customer experience. Based on this chapter, answer the following:

1. Recommend two AI tools or applications that would help streamline inventory management and personalize customer interactions.
2. Discuss one potential privacy concern the retail chain should address when implementing AI-driven systems.
3. Propose a smart consumer-facing feature (e.g., an app or service) that leverages AI to enhance customer loyalty.

Objective: Use real-life examples from this chapter to justify your recommendations.

REFERENCES

- Amazon. (n.d.). *Recommendation Engines and AI in Retail*. Retrieved from Amazon Web Services.
- OpenAI. (n.d.). *AI and Personal Assistants*. Retrieved from OpenAI Blog.
- Tesla. (n.d.). *Autonomous Driving Technology*. Retrieved from Tesla AI.
- Google. (n.d.). *How Google Maps Uses AI for Route Optimization*. Retrieved from Google AI.
- Nest. (n.d.). *AI-Powered Smart Home Solutions*. Retrieved from Nest.

- IBM Watson. (n.d.). *Predictive Analytics in Healthcare*. Retrieved from IBM Watson.

CHAPTER 5: AI AS A COMPETITIVE ADVANTAGE

In today's fast-paced business world, artificial intelligence (AI) has become more than just a trend; it's a critical tool for staying ahead. Companies that successfully harness AI don't just streamline operations—they innovate, predict, and personalize in ways that set them apart. Think of AI as the modern business equivalent of the Swiss Army knife: versatile, indispensable, and capable of solving problems you didn't even know you had. This chapter dives into real-world examples and actionable strategies to help you see how AI can give your business an edge.

How Businesses Are Using AI to Win

AI has transformed industries, creating advantages that were unimaginable a decade ago. Let's look at some standout examples:

AMAZON: PERSONALIZATION MEETS PRECISION

Amazon's secret sauce is its AI-powered recommendation engine, responsible for driving a significant chunk of its sales. By analyzing customer behavior—what you browse, buy, or leave behind in your cart—Amazon personalizes the shopping experience at scale.

- **Dynamic Pricing:** AI adjusts prices in real time based on factors like demand and competitor pricing.

- **Inventory Forecasting:** Machine learning predicts stock needs, reducing waste and out-of-stock scenarios.
- **Efficient Logistics:** From robotic warehouses to AI-optimized delivery routes, Amazon's supply chain hums like a well-oiled machine.

NETFLIX: KEEPING YOU HOOKED

Ever wonder why Netflix always seems to know what you'll enjoy next? AI drives their recommendation system, analyzing everything from your viewing history to how long you pause during a scene.

- **Content Creation:** AI guides decisions on new shows and movies, helping Netflix invest in content that resonates with its audience.
- **Seamless Streaming:** Real-time AI tweaks video quality based on your internet connection, keeping buffering to a minimum.

HEALTHCARE STARTUPS: SPEEDING UP DIAGNOSES

Companies like PathAI and Tempus are leveraging AI to detect diseases earlier and with greater accuracy.

- **Error Reduction:** AI catches anomalies that even seasoned doctors might miss.
- **Accelerated Research:** Analyzing massive datasets in record time, AI identifies trends that push medical research forward.

AI isn't just for the Amazons and Netflixes of the world. Here's how businesses—big and small—can use AI to gain an edge:

1. Data-Driven Decisions

Gone are the days of relying on gut instincts. AI enables smarter decision-making with real-time insights.

- **Predictive Analytics:** AI forecasts market trends, helping you anticipate customer needs.
- **Customer Segmentation:** Identify high-value customers and tailor your marketing to them.

Example: A coffee chain used AI to analyze foot traffic and weather data, adjusting staffing and promotions to boost sales on busy days.

2. Automation to Save Time and Money

AI can take repetitive tasks off your plate, freeing up your team to focus on more strategic work.

- **Customer Service:** Chatbots handle routine inquiries, improving response times.
- **Inventory Management:** AI monitors stock levels and automates reorders.

Example: A manufacturing company reduced production lead times by 25% using AI-driven scheduling software.

AI makes it possible to deliver a tailored experience to every customer without scaling up your resources.

- **Marketing Campaigns:** AI creates hyper-targeted ads based on user behavior.
- **Product Suggestions:** Retailers boost sales by recommending items customers are likely to love.

Example: A local fashion boutique used AI to suggest outfit pairings, increasing repeat purchases by 40%.

4. Sparking Innovation

AI is a powerful tool for uncovering opportunities and driving creativity.

- **Product Development:** Analyze customer feedback to identify new product ideas.
- **Competitive Insights:** AI keeps tabs on competitors, helping you stay one step ahead.

Example: A beverage company used AI to create a new flavor by analyzing social media chatter. The launch became one of their best sellers.

AI for Small Businesses: Leveling the Playing Field

Advanced AI tools are no longer exclusive to industry giants. Many affordable solutions cater specifically to small businesses.

- **Chatbots:** Platforms like ManyChat provide 24/7 support without breaking the bank.
- **Email Marketing:** Tools like Mailchimp's AI recommendations enhance engagement effortlessly.
- **SEO:** AI-powered tools like MarketMuse improve your website's search rankings.

Adopting AI isn't just about cutting costs—it's about creating an experience that's professional and competitive.

Strategic Thinking with AI

AI doesn't just streamline tasks; it helps shape strategy.

- **Market Forecasting:** Predict demand shifts to stay ahead of the curve.
- **Customer Journeys:** Pinpoint friction points and improve the user experience.
- **Risk Management:** AI flags potential risks, from supply chain issues to financial irregularities.

Example: A consulting firm used AI to analyze client data, predicting future needs and improving resource allocation.

Challenges and Considerations

While AI has enormous potential, it comes with hurdles:

- **Implementation Costs:** Initial setup can be pricey.
- **Skill Gaps:** You'll need the right talent to make the most of AI tools.
- **Data Dependency:** Poor data quality leads to poor AI performance.

The key is to balance these challenges with your goals and resources.

Key Takeaways

- AI offers competitive advantages in efficiency, customer engagement, and innovation.
- Businesses of all sizes can benefit by choosing tools and strategies aligned with their needs.
- Success requires clear goals, quality data, and a willingness to adapt.

AI isn't the future—it's the present. By embracing its possibilities today, your business can not only keep up but lead. And as we look ahead, the organizations that leverage AI wisely will set the pace for the industries of tomorrow.

Knowledge Check

This section is designed to assess your understanding of how AI provides competitive advantages in business.

Questions:

1. What drives Amazon's recommendation engine?
   a. Human curation of product listings
   b. AI analyzing customer behavior
   c. Randomized product suggestions
   d. Vendor recommendations
2. True or False: AI is only beneficial for large corporations with significant resources.
3. How does AI help small businesses compete?
   a. By automating routine tasks
   b. By eliminating customer interactions
   c. By creating one-size-fits-all solutions
   d. By reducing the need for marketing
4. Which of the following is NOT an AI-driven strategy mentioned in this chapter?
   a. Predictive analytics
   b. Market forecasting
   c. Inventory monitoring
   d. Business licensing automation
5. Name one challenge of implementing AI in business and propose a potential solution.

Scenario:
You are advising a mid-sized retail business looking to improve efficiency, personalize customer experiences, and innovate their product offerings. Based on this chapter:

1. Identify two specific AI tools or techniques they should implement and explain why.
2. Discuss how they can use AI to optimize inventory management.
3. Suggest one innovative way AI could help the business develop a new product or service.

Objective: Demonstrate how AI can address practical business needs with actionable strategies.

REFERENCES

- OpenAI. (n.d.). *Applications of AI in Business.* Retrieved from OpenAI Blog.
- Amazon. (n.d.). *How AI Powers Amazon's Logistics and Recommendations.* Retrieved from Amazon Web Services.
- Netflix. (n.d.). *AI and Machine Learning in Content Recommendations.* Retrieved from Netflix Tech Blog.
- ManyChat. (n.d.). *AI Chatbots for Small Businesses.* Retrieved from ManyChat.
- IBM Watson. (n.d.). *AI for Inventory Management and Predictive Analytics.* Retrieved from IBM Watson.

- MarketMuse. (n.d.). *SEO Optimization Using AI*. Retrieved from MarketMuse.

Automation's Impact on Employment:

Change can be a formidable adversary for many, particularly when it involves embracing new technology. It is a common phenomenon for people to feel uneasy about stepping out of their comfort zones and learning something entirely new. This resistance often stems from a fear of the unknown, a lack of confidence in one's ability to adapt, and the comfort of familiarity.

One key reason for this resistance is the cognitive and emotional effort required to learn new technology. For instance, individuals may need to invest time and energy into understanding new systems, which can be daunting, especially if they feel their current skills are sufficient. This is compounded by the perception that technology can be complex and ever-changing, making it seem like a moving target that is difficult to keep up with.

Moreover, the fear of failure plays a significant role. People may worry that they will not be able to master the new technology, which could lead to mistakes or decreased productivity. This fear can be particularly pronounced in professional settings, where the stakes are high, and there may be concerns about job security or performance evaluations.

It is also worth noting that some people may have had negative experiences with technology in the past, which can contribute to their reluctance to embrace new tools. These experiences can create a mental block, making it harder for individuals to approach new technology with an open mind.

Despite these challenges, it is important to recognize that learning new technology can be highly beneficial. It can lead to increased efficiency, new opportunities, and a greater sense of accomplishment. Organizations can help ease the transition by providing training, support, and clear communication about the benefits of the new technology.

In conclusion, while it is normal for people to resist change and be apprehensive about learning new technology, understanding the reasons behind this resistance can help in devising strategies to support and encourage individuals through the transition. With the right approach, the journey from resistance to acceptance can be made smoother and more rewarding.

AI and automation are expected to automate certain tasks, leading to the displacement of specific jobs. More recent analyses suggest that high-skilled workers in non-routine jobs are also susceptible to AI automation. For instance, a study by the International Monetary Fund (2020) predicts that AI will affect nearly 40% of jobs, with high-skilled roles in analytical and non-routine tasks being particularly at risk. Additionally, research from Maastricht University (2021) and the Institute for Employment Research (2021) indicates that while automation can augment some high-skilled jobs, it also poses a significant threat to others, potentially leading to wage disparities and job displacement. This highlights the need for continuous skill development and adaptation to remain relevant in an increasingly automated world.

The field of artificial intelligence (AI) is burgeoning with new job opportunities, driven by the increasing adoption of AI across various industries (Coursera, 2025). Projections indicate that roles in AI will continue to grow rapidly, with the U.S. Bureau of Labor Statistics forecasting a 26% increase in computer and information research jobs between 2023 and 2033 (Forbes, 2024).

Companies are actively training their workforce to adapt to AI advancements. Training programs focusing on AI proficiency are becoming more common, helping employees acquire the necessary skills to develop and manage AI systems (Forbes). According to Forbes, corporate AI training programs have evolved to include AI-generated videos, automated test creation, and personalized learning paths, ensuring employees are well-equipped to handle AI technologies efficiently.

Furthermore, many software companies are integrating AI concepts and automation into their existing software. AI automation helps businesses streamline workflows, reduce costs, and improve productivity by handling repetitive tasks and complex workflows (Salesforce). This widespread integration of AI in software signifies a demand for AI-related skills, reinforcing job security for those trained in this area.

In summary, the AI industry not only promises numerous job openings but also ensures job security through continuous learning and adaptation to new AI technologies. This blend of opportunities and ongoing education positions AI professionals for sustained success in the ever-evolving job market.

New Job Roles Emerging from AI:

While automation will undoubtedly affect jobs, it also opens a realm of opportunities for individuals to learn and master new technologies. As industries adopt automated systems and artificial intelligence, the demand for skilled workers who can develop, manage, and maintain these technologies will rise. According to a report by McKinsey & Company, automation could create up to 133 million new roles globally by 2030, offsetting the 75 million jobs that might be displaced.

Moreover, automation has the potential to enhance productivity and efficiency across various sectors. This increased productivity can lead to economic growth and, consequently, the creation of additional job opportunities. For instance, a study by the World Economic Forum indicates that emerging technologies, such as AI and robotics, could generate a net positive job growth of around 58 million jobs worldwide.

Furthermore, as automation takes over repetitive and mundane tasks, workers can focus on more complex and creative aspects of their jobs. This shift not only enriches job satisfaction but also fosters innovation and personal development. The MIT Task Force on the Work of the Future highlights that while some job categories may decline, others will emerge, necessitating upskilling and reskilling efforts to ensure that the workforce can transition into these new roles.

In summary, while automation will impact certain job sectors, it also offers substantial opportunities for learning new technologies, creating new roles, and enhancing existing ones. This dynamic change underscores the importance of continuous education and training to adapt to the evolving job market.

The Balance Between Human Skills and Machine Intelligence:

While AI and ML are helping us in so many areas, there are situations where we should not depend on these technologies 100%. A human expert must oversee the medical procedures or sensitive missions.

It is crucial to recognize that while artificial intelligence (AI) and machine learning (ML) have revolutionized various sectors, including healthcare and military operations, their limitations necessitate human oversight to ensure accuracy and ethical standards.

In the medical field, AI and ML have immensely contributed to advancements in diagnostics and treatment plans. For example, AI algorithms can analyze vast amounts of medical data to identify patterns that human doctors might overlook. These technologies have been instrumental in early disease detection, personalized medicine, and predictive analytics. However, the complexity and variability of human biology mean that AI's interpretations might not always be accurate. There is also the issue of algorithmic bias, where AI systems may produce skewed results due to biased training data. Thus, leaving critical decisions solely to AI systems could lead to serious consequences if the algorithm fails to account for unique patient circumstances. Therefore, human experts are essential to review AI recommendations and apply their judgment and experience.

in sensitive missions, such as military operations, while AI-powered drones and surveillance systems enhance efficiency and reduce human risk, they also pose significant ethical and decision-making challenges. Autonomous systems can execute tasks without human intervention, but they lack the nuanced understanding of context and ethics that humans possess. For instance, an AI drone might identify a target based on pre-programmed parameters, but it cannot comprehend the broader political and humanitarian implications of its actions. Human oversight ensures that such decisions consider the ethical dimensions and potential consequences beyond what AI can foresee.

In conclusion, while AI and ML offer remarkable benefits, their integration into critical sectors like healthcare and military operations must be balanced with human oversight to mitigate risks and uphold ethical standards. This blended approach leverages the strengths of both AI and human expertise to achieve optimal outcomes.

Chapter 6 Summary Diagram:

Topic	Positive	Negative
Automation's Impact on Employment	Increased efficiency, new opportunities, and a greater sense of accomplishment in learning AI. Projections indicate that roles in AI will continue to grow. Corporate AI training programs have evolved to include AI-generated videos, automated test creation, and personalized learning paths.	Change due to learning AI AI will affect nearly 40% of jobs Wage disparities and job displacement

	Companies are integrating AI concepts and automation into their existing software.	
New Job Roles Emerging from AI	Opens a realm of opportunities Enhance productivity and efficiency Can focus on more complex and creative aspects of jobs	Affect jobs Takes over repetitive and mundane tasks
The Balance Between Human Skills and Machine Intelligence	A human expert must oversee the medical procedures or sensitive missions. AI and ML have immensely	We should not depend on these technologies 100%. Limitations necessitate

contributed to advancements in diagnostics and treatment plans in healthcare. In military operations, AI-powered drones and surveillance systems enhance efficiency and reduce human risk	human oversight to ensure accuracy and ethical standards Cannot comprehend the broader political and humanitarian implications

Knowledge Check:
Exercise "Automation's Impact on Employment"

1. What is one reason for resistance to adopting new technology mentioned in the text?

A) The lack of available jobs in the tech industry

B) The high cost of acquiring new technology

C) The cognitive and emotional effort required to learn new technology

D) The abundance of resources and support available for training

2. According to recent analyses, which group of workers is susceptible to AI automation?

A) Low-skilled workers in routine jobs

B) High-skilled workers in non-routine jobs

C) Mid-skilled workers in manual labor

D) Entry-level workers in customer service

Exercise "New Job Roles Emerging from AI"

3. According to McKinsey & Company, how many new roles could automation create globally by 2030?

A) 50 million

B) 100 million

C) 133 million

D) 150 million

4. What is one of the potential benefits of automation highlighted in the text?

A) Increased job dissatisfaction

B) Higher costs for companies

C) Focus on complex and creative tasks

D) Decreased need for worker upskilling

Exercise "The Balance Between Human Skills and Machine Intelligence"

5. Why is human oversight essential in medical procedures involving AI and ML?

A) To reduce the cost of medical treatments

B) Because AI systems always produce accurate results

C) To ensure ethical standards and accuracy

D) To avoid using technology in healthcare altogether

6. What is one of the challenges of using AI in sensitive military missions?

A) AI systems always operate independently without a need for human input

B) AI lacks the nuanced understanding of context and ethics

C) AI systems are more expensive than human soldiers

D) AI can only be used in non-combat scenarios

CITATIONS:
Chockley, K., & Emanuel, E. (2016). The End of Radiology? Three Threats to the Future Practice of Radiology. *Journal of the American College of Radiology, 13*(12), 1415–1420.

Coursera. (2025). *6 Artificial Intelligence (AI) Jobs to Consider in 2025.*

Forbes. (2024). *10 Trends In AI Corporate Employee Training As We Move Toward 2025.*

Institute for Employment Research. (2021). *Automation and the Future of Work: The Impact on High-Skilled Workers.*

International Monetary Fund. (2020). *The Impact of Artificial Intelligence on Employment.*

Maastricht University. (2021). *The Future of Work: How AI Will Transform High-Skilled Jobs.*

McKinsey & Company. (2017). *Jobs Lost, Jobs Gained: Workforce Transitions in a Time*

   of Automation. Retrieved from McKinsey & Company

MIT Task Force on the Work of the Future. (2019). *Work of the Future: Shaping*

   Technology and Institutions. Retrieved from MIT

Topol, E. (2019). *Deep Medicine: How Artificial Intelligence Can Make Healthcare*

   Human Again. New York: Basic Books.

World Economic Forum. (2018). *The Future of Jobs Report 2018.* Retrieved from World

   Economic Forum

CHAPTER 7: IMPORTANCE OF DATA IN AI

Data as the Fuel of AI Systems

The advent of artificial intelligence (AI) and machine learning (ML) has significantly augmented the importance of data in technological processes. Traditionally, computers were primarily used for data processing, executing predefined instructions to manipulate and store information. However, with the emergence of AI and ML, data has evolved from being merely a processed entity to becoming the fundamental driving force behind intelligent decision-making systems. In essence, data serves as the fuel of AI systems, enabling them to learn, adapt, and make informed decisions.

Data as the Backbone of AI Systems

Data plays a pivotal role in the functioning of AI systems by providing the foundation on which these systems operate. AI and ML algorithms rely heavily on large volumes of data to understand patterns, make predictions, and generate insights. For instance, a machine learning model designed to recognize images must be trained on thousands, if not millions, of labeled images to accurately identify objects.

The quality, quantity, and diversity of the data directly impact the model's performance and accuracy. High-quality data ensures that the AI system can learn effectively and make reliable predictions, while diverse datasets help the system generalize better across different scenarios.

Moreover, data is essential for training AI models in various domains, including natural language processing, computer vision, and recommendation systems. In natural language processing, AI models are trained on extensive text corpora to understand and generate human language. Similarly, computer vision models require large datasets of labeled images or videos to recognize and interpret visual content. Recommendation systems, like those used by streaming services and e-commerce platforms, leverage user data to personalize content and improve user experience. Without access to vast amounts of data, these AI models would struggle to achieve high levels of accuracy and utility.

The Role of Data in Enhancing AI Capabilities

Beyond training, data continues to be crucial throughout the AI lifecycle, including validation, testing, and real-world deployment. During validation, datasets are used to fine-tune AI models and identify potential biases or inaccuracies. Testing involves evaluating the model's performance on unseen data to ensure its robustness and generalization capabilities. Continuous data collection and analysis help maintain AI systems' effectiveness and adaptability in real-world applications.

In healthcare, for example, AI-driven diagnostic tools rely on patient data to provide accurate diagnoses and treatment recommendations. These tools can analyze medical records, imaging data, and genetic information to identify patterns and anomalies that may indicate potential health issues. However, the success of these AI systems depends on the availability of comprehensive and high-quality medical data. Inadequate or biased data can lead to incorrect diagnoses or treatment plans, highlighting the importance of robust data collection and management practices.

Data Quality and Ethical Considerations

The importance of data quality in AI systems cannot be overstated. Poor-quality data, including incomplete, outdated, or biased datasets, can significantly hamper the performance of AI models. Ensuring data quality involves rigorous data cleaning, preprocessing, and augmentation processes to eliminate errors and inconsistencies. Additionally, diverse, and representative datasets are critical to mitigating biases and ensuring that AI systems are fair and unbiased. Bias in AI can arise from skewed data, which may disproportionately represent certain groups or fail to capture the full spectrum of real-world scenarios.

Ethical considerations in data management are paramount to the responsible development and deployment of AI systems. Issues such as data privacy, consent, and transparency must be addressed to uphold ethical standards and build trust with users. For instance, in all applications without any exceptions especially personal data used in healthcare AI applications must be handled with strict confidentiality and compliance with data protection regulations. Ethical data practices also involve transparency in data sources, data usage, and the decision-making processes of AI systems, allowing users to understand and trust AI-driven outcomes.

The Role of Big Data and Data Analytics

The rise of big data has further amplified the importance of data in AI systems. Big data refers to the massive volumes of structured and unstructured data generated by various sources, including social media, sensors, and online transactions. The ability to harness and analyze this data is crucial for developing sophisticated AI models. Data analytics techniques, such as data mining, clustering, and predictive analytics, help uncover valuable insights from big data, informing AI-driven decision-making processes.

For example, in the retail sector, big data analytics enables businesses to understand consumer behavior, optimize inventory management, and personalize marketing strategies. By analyzing data from customer interactions, purchase history, and social media activity, AI systems can generate actionable insights that drive business growth and enhance customer satisfaction. The synergy between big data and AI underscores the importance of robust data infrastructure and advanced data analytics capabilities.

The Future of Data-Driven AI

The future of AI is inherently tied to advancements in data collection, storage, and processing technologies. Innovations such as edge computing, distributed data platforms, and blockchain are poised to enhance data management and security, fueling the next generation of AI systems.

Edge computing is a decentralized computing paradigm that brings data storage and computation closer to the location where it is needed, rather than relying solely on a centralized data center. This approach aims to reduce latency, improve real-time processing, and enhance the overall performance of applications and services. By processing data at the "edge" of the network, closer to the source of data generation (such as smart devices, sensors, and IoT nodes), edge computing minimizes the time it takes for data to travel back and forth between the device and the central cloud. Edge computing enables data processing at the source, reducing latency and improving real-time decision-making capabilities. Distributed data platforms facilitate the seamless integration and analysis of data from multiple sources, enhancing AI models scalability and flexibility.

Blockchain (the technology behind Bitcoin), with its decentralized and immutable ledger, offers a promising solution for secure and transparent data transactions. By ensuring data integrity and traceability, blockchain can address ethical concerns related to data privacy and consent. Integrating these technologies with AI systems will pave the way for more resilient, trustworthy, and efficient AI applications across various domains.

In conclusion, data is the lifeblood of AI systems, driving their learning, adaptability, and decision-making capabilities. The quality, diversity, and ethical management of data are crucial to the success and reliability of AI applications. As AI continues to evolve and permeate various industries, the importance of robust data practices becomes even more critical. Embracing advancements in data technologies will unlock new possibilities and ensure that AI systems remain effective, ethical, and impactful in addressing global challenges and opportunities.

Data Collection, Cleaning, and Processing:

In the realm of artificial intelligence (AI) and machine learning (ML), the journey from raw data to actionable insights is underpinned by three crucial steps: data collection, data cleaning, and data processing. These steps ensure that data fed into AI systems is accurate, reliable, and ready for sophisticated analysis and decision-making.

Data Collection: Laying the Foundation

Data collection is the first and arguably the most critical step in the data processing pipeline. This phase involves gathering raw data from various sources, such as sensors, databases, user interactions, social media, and other digital platforms. The quality of data collected is paramount, as it forms the foundation upon which AI models are built.

Several key properties define effective data collection:

1. **Honesty**: Honest data represents truthful and unbiased information. This means collecting data that accurately reflects the real-world scenario it aims to model. For instance, in healthcare, honest

data encompasses accurate medical records and patient histories.

2. **Accuracy**: Accurate data provides precise and correct details. Inaccurate data can lead to erroneous AI predictions and decisions. Ensuring data accuracy involves validation checks, cross-referencing with reliable sources, and periodic updates.

3. **Relevance**: Relevant data pertains directly to the application at hand. Collecting data that is closely aligned with the problem being solved ensures that AI models receive the most pertinent information for training and analysis.

Effective data collection methods involve employing various technologies and strategies, such as automated data scraping, Internet of Things (IoT) devices, and user feedback systems. These methods help gather comprehensive datasets that encompass diverse scenarios and conditions.

Data Cleaning: Ensuring Quality and Integrity

Once data is collected, it undergoes a meticulous cleaning process. Raw data often contains errors, inconsistencies, and irrelevant information that can compromise the quality of AI models. Data cleaning aims to rectify these issues and produce a clean, usable dataset.

STEPS INVOLVED IN DATA CLEANING:

1. **Error Detection and Correction**: Identifying and correcting erroneous values is the first step in data cleaning. This process involves detecting outliers, validating data against known standards, and correcting typographical errors.

2. **Handling Missing Data**: Incomplete data can skew analysis and predictions. Strategies for handling missing data include imputation (replacing missing values with estimated ones), deletion (removing incomplete records), or using algorithms that can handle missing data.

3. **Removing Duplicates**: Duplicate entries can lead to biased analysis and redundant information.

identifying and removing duplicates ensures that each data point is represented only once.

4. **Standardization**: Ensuring consistency in data formatting is crucial. Standardization involves converting data into a common format, such as using consistent date formats, unit measurements, and categorical representations.

5. **Bias Mitigation**: Bias in data can lead to unfair and inaccurate AI predictions. Cleaning data to ensure it fairly represents all relevant groups and scenarios is essential for developing unbiased AI models.

Data Processing: Transforming Data for Analysis

Following data collection and cleaning, the next step is data processing. This phase involves transforming raw data into a format suitable for analysis by AI models. Data processing includes normalization, standardization, and feature extraction, which enhance the quality and effectiveness of AI training.

KEY STEPS IN DATA PROCESSING:
1. **Normalization**: Normalization scales data to a consistent range, typically between 0 and 1. This

step ensures that all features contribute equally to the model's learning process, preventing any single feature from dominating due to its large scale.

2. **Standardization**: Standardization adjusts data to have a mean of zero and a standard deviation of one. This ensures that data distributions are comparable and improves the stability and performance of AI models.

3. **Feature Extraction**: Feature extraction involves identifying and selecting the most relevant variables (features) from the dataset. Effective feature extraction enhances model accuracy and reduces computational complexity by focusing on the most informative aspects of the data.

Ensuring Data Quality and Ethical Considerations

The importance of data quality in AI systems cannot be overstated. Poor-quality data, including incomplete, outdated, or biased datasets, can significantly hamper the performance of AI models. Ensuring data quality involves rigorous data cleaning, preprocessing, and augmentation processes to eliminate errors and inconsistencies.

Additionally, diverse, and representative datasets are critical to mitigating biases and ensuring that AI systems are fair and unbiased. Bias in AI can arise from skewed data, which may disproportionately represent certain groups or fail to capture the full spectrum of real-world scenarios.

Ethical considerations in data management are paramount to the responsible development and deployment of AI systems. Issues such as data privacy, consent, and transparency must be addressed to uphold ethical standards and build trust with users. For instance, personal data used in healthcare AI applications must be handled with strict confidentiality and compliance with data protection regulations. Ethical data practices also involve transparency in data sources, data usage, and the decision-making processes of AI systems, allowing users to understand and trust AI-driven outcomes.

The Role of Big Data and Data Analytics

Big data has further enlarged the importance AI systems. Big data can be defined as the massive volumes of data generated by various sources which could be due to high speed or other resources. It includes social media, sensors of aircrafts, and massive online transactions of the e-Commerce sites. The ability to harness and analyze this data is crucial for developing sophisticated AI models.

DATA ANALYTICS TECHNIQUES, SUCH AS:

Data mining: Involves discovering patterns and relationships within large datasets, uncovering hidden insights that inform AI models' decision-making.

Clustering: Grouping similar data points together to identify patterns is exhibited across different subsets of data.

Predictive analytics: Leveraging historical data to predict future trends and outcomes enables AI systems to make informed decisions based on past patterns. In the retail sector, for example, big data analytics enables businesses to understand consumer behavior, optimize inventory management, and personalize marketing strategies. By analyzing data from customer interactions, purchase history, and social media activity, AI systems can generate actionable insights that drive business growth and enhance customer satisfaction.

Ensuring Data Quality & Integrity

The synergy between big data and AI underscores the importance of robust data infrastructure and advanced data analytics capabilities. Handling large-scale data efficiently demands advanced data processing techniques and tools, as well as a coordinated effort to ensure data quality, integrity, and ethical compliance.

THE FUTURE OF DATA-DRIVEN AI

The future of AI is inherently tied to advancements in data collection, storage, and processing technologies. Innovations such as edge computing, distributed data platforms, and blockchain are poised to enhance data management and security, fueling the next generation of AI systems. Edge computing enables data processing at the source, reducing latency and improving real-time decision-making capabilities. Distributed data platforms facilitate the seamless integration and analysis of data from multiple sources, enhancing AI models' scalability and flexibility.

Blockchain technology, with its decentralized and immutable ledger, offers a promising solution for secure and transparent data transactions. By ensuring data integrity and traceability, blockchain can address ethical concerns related to data privacy and consent. Integrating these technologies with AI systems will pave the way for more resilient, trustworthy, and efficient AI applications across various domains.

In conclusion, data collection, data cleaning, and data processing form the backbone of effective AI systems. Each step is vital in ensuring that the data used is accurate, reliable, and suitable for analysis. By adhering to rigorous data practices and embracing advancements in data technologies, the future of AI will be marked by greater efficiency, ethical integrity, and transformative potential.

DATA PRIVACY AND SECURITY CONCERNS:

In the age of digital transformation, data privacy and security concerns have increasingly become pivotal issues. As organizations collect, process, and leverage vast amounts of data to drive business strategies and enhance customer experiences, the need to protect sensitive information from breaches and misuse is more critical than ever. Good data processing, which includes steps such as data collection, cleaning, and processing, forms the foundation of this protection, ensuring integrity and trust in the data lifecycle. This chapter delves into the complexities of data privacy and security, emphasizing the importance of these practices and exploring various dimensions of safeguarding data.

DATA PRIVACY AND ITS SIGNIFICANCE

Data privacy refers to the proper handling, processing, storage, and use of personal information. It ensures that individuals' data is collected and processed with their consent and used in ways that align with their expectations. The significance of data privacy lies in its ability to protect individuals from unauthorized access and potential misuse of their personal information. This protection extends to various sectors, including finance, healthcare, and social media, where sensitive data is routinely handled.

One key aspect of data privacy is the principle of consent. Users must be informed about how their data will be used and have the right to opt-in or opt-out of data collection practices. Transparency in data practices fosters trust between users and organizations, ensuring that individuals feel secure in sharing their information.

Moreover, data privacy regulations, such as the General Data Protection Regulation (GDPR) in Europe and the California Consumer Privacy Act (CCPA) in the United States, have been established to safeguard individuals' privacy rights. These regulations mandate strict guidelines for data collection, processing, and storage, holding organizations accountable for their data practices.

CHALLENGES IN DATA PRIVACY

Despite the robust framework of regulations, organizations face several challenges in ensuring data privacy:

1. **Data Breaches**: One of the most significant challenges is preventing data breaches. Cybercriminals continually evolve their tactics, seeking vulnerabilities in systems to gain unauthorized access to sensitive information. Data breaches can result in severe financial, legal, and reputational damage to organizations and compromise individuals' privacy.

2. **Data Misuse**: Another challenge is preventing data misuse. Even within an organization, employees with access to sensitive information may misuse

data, either intentionally or unintentionally. Implementing strict access controls and monitoring mechanisms is crucial to mitigate this risk.

3. **Compliance**: Adhering to data privacy regulations is complex and resource-intensive. Organizations must invest in compliance programs to ensure they meet regulatory requirements and avoid penalties. This includes regular audits, policy updates, and employee training.

Principles of Data Security

Data security encompasses the measures taken to protect data from unauthorized access, corruption, or theft throughout its lifecycle. Effective data security practices ensure the confidentiality, integrity, and availability of data. Key principles of data security include:

1. **Confidentiality**: Ensuring that sensitive information is accessible only to authorized individuals and entities. Confidentiality measures include encryption, access controls, and secure communication protocols.

2. **Integrity**: Maintaining the accuracy and reliability of data. Integrity measures protect against data tampering, ensuring that data remains unchanged during storage and transmission.

3. **Availability**: Ensuring that data is accessible when needed. Availability measures include redundant systems, backup strategies, and disaster recovery plans to prevent data loss and downtime.

Ethical Considerations and Challenges

Ensuring data privacy and security involves addressing several ethical considerations and challenges:

1. **Data Privacy**: Organizations must ensure that personal data is handled with strict confidentiality and in compliance with data protection regulations. Ethical data practices involve transparency in data sources, data usage, and AI decision-making processes.

2. **Data Security**: Implementing robust security measures, such as encryption and access controls, to protect data from unauthorized access and breaches.

3. **Bias and Fairness**. Ensuring the AI models and analyses are free from biases that could result in unfair treatment of individuals or groups. This involves rigorous data cleaning and preprocessing to mitigate potential biases.

4. **Transparency and Accountability**: Maintaining transparency in data practices and holding organizations accountable for any breaches or misuse of data. This includes regular audits, policy updates, and public disclosures.

CHAPTER 7 SUMMARY DIAGRAM:

Importance of Data in AI	Main Points
Data as the Fuel of AI Systems	Data is the backbone of AI Systems Data Considerations & Ethical aspects Big Data & Analytics

119

Data Collection, Cleaning, and Processing	Data collection is the foundation (Honesty, Accuracy, Relevance) Data Cleaning: Ensuring Quality and Integrity Data Processing: Transforming Data for Analysis
Data Privacy and Security	Challenges in Data Privacy (Data Breaches, Data Compliance, Data Misuse) Principles of Data Security (Confidentiality, Integrity, Availability) Ethical Considerations and Challenges (Data Privacy, Data Security, Bias and

	Fairness, Transparency & Accountability)

Knowledge Check:

Question 1:

What role does data play in the functioning of AI systems?

A. Data is only used for storing information.

B. Data provides the foundation for AI to learn, adapt, and make informed decisions.

C. Data is optional for training AI systems.

D. Data is only needed during the testing phase of AI systems.

Question 2:

What is a critical factor in ensuring the effectiveness of AI-driven decision-making systems?

A. High volumes of unprocessed data.

B. Data quality, diversity, and ethical management.

C. Exclusive reliance on structured datasets.

D. Minimizing the use of data in AI applications.

Question 3:

What is the primary purpose of the data cleaning process

in the data processing pipeline?

A. Collecting raw data from various sources.

B. Rectifying errors, inconsistencies, and irrelevant information in raw data.

C. Scaling data to a consistent range between 0 and 1.

D. Grouping similar data points to identify patterns.

Question 4:

Which of the following best describes feature extraction in the context of data processing?

A. Removing duplicate entries from the dataset.

B. Selecting the most relevant variables to enhance model accuracy and reduce complexity.

C. Ensuring data distributions are comparable by adjusting the mean and standard deviation.

D. Scaling data to prevent any single feature from dominating due to its large scale.

Question 5:

What is the primary goal of data privacy?

A. Maximizing the amount of data collected by organizations.

B. Ensuring data is accessible to everyone at any time.

C. Protecting individuals' personal information through

proper handling, consent, and regulatory compliance.

D. Allowing organizations to use personal data without restrictions.

Question 6:

Which principle of data security ensures that sensitive information is accessible only to authorized individuals?

A. Integrity

B. Confidentiality

C. Availability

D. Transparency

REFERENCES:
1. Topol, E. (2019). Deep Medicine: How Artificial Intelligence Can Make Healthcare Human Again. New York: Basic Books.

2. McKinsey & Company. (2017). Jobs Lost, Jobs Gained: Workforce Transitions in a Time of Automation. Retrieved from McKinsey & Company.

AI for Augmented Decision Making:

Artificial Intelligence (AI) has the remarkable capability to make informed decisions by processing vast amounts of data and identifying patterns that may not be immediately apparent to human analysts. This ability to analyze large datasets is particularly advantageous in environments where the sheer volume of information can be overwhelming for human decision-makers. AI systems excel in such scenarios because they can quickly and efficiently sift through data to provide insights and recommendations based on objective analysis (Domingos, 2015).

One of the primary strengths of AI in decision-making is its objectivity. Unlike humans, AI is not influenced by emotions, biases, or external pressures, which can often skew judgment. This objectivity ensures that decisions are based purely on data-driven evidence, leading to potentially more accurate outcomes, especially when dealing with vast datasets. For instance, in the field of healthcare, AI is being utilized to analyze medical records and research data to diagnose diseases, suggest treatments, and even predict patient outcomes (Topol, 2019). By identifying patterns and correlations within extensive medical databases, AI can assist physicians in making more accurate diagnoses and personalized treatment plans.

In contrast, when the dataset is small or the number of variables is limited, human decision-making often proves faster and potentially more accurate. Humans can leverage their intuition, experience, and contextual understanding to make decisions in situations where AI might struggle due to the lack of extensive data. For example, in a small business setting, an entrepreneur might rely on their personal experiences and industry knowledge to make quick decisions about product launches or marketing strategies. This type of decision-making benefits from the nuanced understanding that humans bring to the table, something that AI may not be able to replicate with limited data inputs.

However, as the complexity and volume of data increase, the advantages of AI become more pronounced. In fields such as finance, AI algorithms are used to analyze market trends, forecast economic conditions, and manage millions of data points from diverse sources, far exceeding the capabilities of human analysts. By identifying subtle patterns and predicting market movements, AI can help investors make more informed decisions and optimize their financial strategies.

Moreover, AI's potential to reduce errors is another significant benefit. Human decision-making is prone to errors due to fatigue, information overload, and cognitive biases. In contrast, AI systems can maintain consistent performance and accuracy over lengthy periods, making them ideal for tasks that require high precision and reliability. For example, in manufacturing, AI-powered robots are employed to perform repetitive tasks with precision and consistency, significantly reducing the likelihood of defects and improving overall productivity.

Additionally, AI can enhance decision-making in real-time situations where rapid analysis and response are crucial. In cybersecurity, for instance, AI-driven systems can detect and respond to threats much faster than human analysts. By continuously monitoring network traffic and identifying sensitive data and prevent cyber-attacks effectively.

Furthermore, the integration of AI in decision-making processes allows for continuous learning and improvement. Machine learning algorithms can adapt and refine their models based on new data, leading to progressively better performance over time. This iterative learning process enables AI to stay relevant and effective even as conditions change and new data becomes available.

However, it is important to acknowledge that AI is not without its challenges and limitations. One major concern is the potential for algorithmic bias, where AI systems inadvertently perpetuate or amplify existing biases present in the training data. Ensuring the fairness and transparency of AI decision-making processes is a critical area of ongoing research and development. Additionally, the ethical implications of AI decisions, such as in autonomous vehicles or criminal justice algorithms, require careful consideration and oversight to prevent unintended consequences.

In conclusion, AI's ability to process vast amounts of data and identify patterns offers significant advantages in decision-making scenarios involving large datasets and complex variables. By providing objective, data-driven insights, AI can enhance accuracy, reduce errors, and optimize performance across various fields. However, human intuition and contextual understanding remain valuable in situations where data is limited and rapid judgment is required. The optimal use of AI lies in recognizing its strengths and limitations and integrating it effectively with human expertise to achieve the best outcomes (Domingos, 2015; Topol, 2019).

Steps Involved in AI Augmented Decision Making

1. **Problem Definition and Objective Setting**: The first step in AI-augmented decision-making involves clearly defining the problem that needs to be addressed and setting specific objectives. This includes understanding the context, constraints, and desired outcomes. For example, a company might seek to optimize its supply chain efficiency

by reducing delivery times and minimizing costs. Clearly outlining these goals helps in developing an AI solution tailored to meet these objectives.

2. **Data Collection and Preparation**: Once the problem is defined, the next step involves gathering relevant data from various sources. This data may include structured data, such as sales records and customer information, as well as unstructured data, like social media posts and customer reviews. Data collection also involves ensuring the quality and integrity of the data by cleaning it, handling missing values, and removing duplicates. This step is crucial as it lays the foundation for accurate and reliable AI models.

3. **Feature Engineering and Selection**: In this phase, data scientists transform raw data into meaningful features that can be used to train AI models. Feature engineering involves selecting, creating, and transforming variables to enhance the performance of machine learning algorithms. For instance, in a predictive maintenance scenario, features such as machine temperature, vibration

levels, and usage hours might be engineered from raw sensor data to predict equipment failures. Feature selection involves identifying the most relevant features, reducing the dimensionality of the dataset, and improving model efficiency.

4. **Model Selection and Training**: Selecting the appropriate AI model is a critical step in the decision-making process. Various machine learning algorithms, such as decision trees, neural networks, and support vector machines, can be considered based on the specific problem and data characteristics. Once a model is selected, it is trained using historical data to learn patterns and relationships. Training involves adjusting model parameters to minimize errors and improve predictive accuracy. This process may require multiple iterations and parameter tuning to achieve the desired performance.

5. **Model Evaluation and Validation**: After training, the model's performance is evaluated using validation techniques, such as cross-validation and hold-out testing. This step involves assessing the

model's accuracy, precision, recall, and other relevant metrics to ensure it meets the required standards. Evaluating the model on different datasets helps identify potential overfitting or underfitting issues, ensuring its robustness and generalizability to new, unseen data.

6. **Integration and Deployment**: Once the AI model is validated, it is integrated into the decision-making workflow. This step involves deploying the model in a production environment where it can analyze real-time data and provide insights or recommendations. Integration may require collaboration with IT teams to ensure seamless implementation within existing systems and databases. For instance, in a financial institution, an AI model predicting loan defaults might be integrated into the loan approval process to assist underwriters in making informed decisions.

7. **Monitoring and Maintenance**: After deployment, the AI model requires continuous monitoring to ensure its performance remains consistent and reliable. This involves tracking key metrics, such as

deviations or anomalies. Regular maintenance, such as retraining the model with updated data and fine-tuning parameters, is essential to adapt to changing conditions and maintain its efficacy over time.

8. **Human-AI Collaboration**: In AI-augmented decision-making, collaboration between human experts and AI systems is vital. Humans provide context, domain knowledge, and interpretability to the AI-generated insights, ensuring that decisions align with organizational goals and ethical standards (Ransbotham et al., 2017). For example, in a medical diagnosis scenario, AI can assist doctors by highlighting potential diagnoses and treatment options, but the final decision remains with the healthcare professional.

Predictive Analytics and Its Applications:

Predictive analytics has garnered immense attention and critical importance in today's data-driven world. Utilizing statistical algorithms, historical data, and machine learning techniques, predictive analytics forecasts future events and trends, guiding decision-making and strategy formulation. AI significantly enhances predictive analytics, enabling more accurate and efficient predictions across various domains.

One of the most notable areas where predictive analytics, bolstered by AI, is leveraged is the stock market. Investors, financial analysts, and fund managers employ predictive models to anticipate market trends, identify lucrative investment opportunities, and mitigate potential risks. By analyzing vast datasets, including historical stock prices, trading volumes, economic indicators, and news sentiment, AI-powered predictive analytics produces insights about future market behaviors, aiding stakeholders in making informed investment decisions. For instance, natural language processing (NLP) algorithms can analyze news headlines and social media posts to gauge public sentiment and predict stock price movements accordingly. Additionally, machine learning models like neural networks and support vector machines can recognize complex patterns and relationships within the data, providing more accurate forecasts.

in the healthcare sector, predictive analytics powered by AI plays a crucial role that often has life-or-death implications. Developing predictive models in healthcare involves analyzing diverse datasets such as electronic health records, genetic information, and clinical trial data to identify patterns and predict patient outcomes. AI enhances this process by rapidly processing large volumes of data and uncovering subtle correlations that may go unnoticed by human analysts. For example, predictive analytics can determine patients at high risk for chronic diseases like diabetes or heart disease, allowing for early interventions and personalized treatment plans ((Domingos, 2015). AI algorithms can also predict patient readmissions, helping healthcare providers to improve patient outcomes and allocate resources more effectively.

Furthermore, predictive analytics is instrumental in the development and administration of medications. By analyzing patient data, AI can predict responses to specific treatments, minimize adverse effects, and increase the likelihood of successful outcomes. In oncology, for instance, machine learning models can identify which cancer patients are likely to respond to chemotherapies based on their genetic profiles and treatment histories. This allows for more targeted and effective treatment plans, tailored to individual patient needs. Additionally, predictive analytics aids in optimizing hospital operations by forecasting patient admissions, managing bed occupancy, and ensuring adequate staffing levels, ultimately improving healthcare delivery, and reducing costs.

Another critical domain where AI-driven predictive analytics has a profound impact is weather prediction. Accurate weather forecasts can save lives by providing timely warnings of severe weather events such as hurricanes, tornadoes, snow storms, and floods. Predictive models in meteorology analyze historical weather data, satellite imagery, and atmospheric conditions to forecast weather patterns and anticipate extreme events. AI enhances these models by processing vast datasets more efficiently and improving the accuracy of predictions. For instance, AI algorithms can identify early warning signs of hurricanes and predict their path, enabling authorities to take preventive measures and evacuate residents in a timely manner.

In the context of transportation, AI-driven predictive analytics is essential for ensuring safety and efficiency. Weather conditions significantly impact road and air travel, accurate predictions enable better planning and risk management. Airlines rely on weather forecasts to plan flight routes, avoid turbulence, and ensure passenger safety. Similarly, road transport authorities use weather predictions to manage traffic, deploy snowplows during winter storms, and prevent accidents. AI enhances these predictive models by providing more accurate and timely forecasts, allowing for better decision-making and resource allocation.

Besides stock market forecasting, healthcare, and weather prediction, AI-powered predictive analytics extends its benefits to other fields such as supply chain management, retail, and energy. In supply chain management, predictive models can forecast demand, optimize inventory levels, and reduce operational costs. Retailers use predictive analytics to understand customer behavior, personalize marketing campaigns, and enhance customer satisfaction. In the energy sector, predictive analytics helps manage energy consumption, predict equipment failures, and optimize grid operations.

Despite the immense potential of predictive analytics, its effectiveness hinges on the quality and quantity of data used. Incomplete or inaccurate data can lead to erroneous predictions, emphasizing the need for robust data collection and management practices. Additionally, developing accurate predictive models requires expertise in data science and domain knowledge. AI plays a pivotal role in addressing these challenges by automating data processing, improving model accuracy, and enabling continuous learning and adaptation.

AI's ability to enhance predictive analytics is further exemplified in personalized marketing and fraud detection. In personalized marketing, AI-driven predictive models analyze customer data to predict future purchasing behaviors, enabling businesses to tailor their marketing strategies and improve customer engagement. For instance, e-commerce platforms employ AI algorithms to recommend products based on users' browsing and purchase histories, thereby increasing sales and customer satisfaction.

in fraud detection, AI-powered predictive analytics plays a crucial role in identifying suspicious activities and preventing financial losses. By analyzing transaction data, AI models can detect patterns indicative of fraudulent behavior and flag potential threats in real time. This enhances the ability of financial institutions to respond swiftly to security breaches and protect their customers' assets.

Moreover, AI-driven predictive analytics contributes to environmental sustainability by optimizing resource usage and minimizing waste. In agriculture, predictive models analyze weather data, soil conditions, and crop performance to forecast yields and recommend optimal planting and harvesting times. This helps farmers improve productivity and reduce the environmental impact of their practices. Similarly, in energy management, AI predicts energy consumption patterns and optimizes the operation of renewable energy sources, contributing to a more sustainable energy future.

However, the integration of AI in predictive analytics also raises ethical and legal considerations. Ensuring the fairness, transparency, and accountability of AI-driven predictions is vital to prevent biases and unintended consequences. For instance, in healthcare, predictive models must be rigorously tested and validated to ensure they do not inadvertently disadvantage certain groups of patients. Likewise, in the financial sector, maintaining the integrity and privacy of customer data is paramount to building trust in AI-driven solutions.

In conclusion, AI significantly enhances the capabilities of predictive analytics across diverse domains, from stock market forecasting and healthcare to weather prediction and beyond. By leveraging AI, organizations can make more accurate and efficient predictions, leading to better decision-making and improved outcomes. The combination of AI and predictive analytics offers a powerful tool for addressing complex challenges and driving innovation in various fields. Nevertheless, ethical considerations and data quality remain critical to harnessing the full potential of AI-driven predictive analytics while ensuring fairness and accountability (Domingos, 2015).

Artificial Intelligence (AI) has been a game-changer in augmenting decision-making and predictive analytics, offering unprecedented capabilities to both small businesses and large enterprises. By leveraging AI, businesses can harness the power of data to make more informed, timely, and accurate decisions, ultimately improving their competitiveness and operational efficiency.

One of the key areas where AI has made a significant impact is in financial decision-making. Financial analysts and executives often rely on AI-driven tools to analyze vast amounts of financial data, identify patterns, and generate insights that would be impossible to discern manually. For instance, predictive analytics can help businesses forecast revenue, optimize budget allocations, and manage risks more effectively. AI algorithms can process historical financial data, market trends, and economic indicators to predict future financial performance, enabling businesses to make strategic decisions with greater confidence. This is particularly valuable for small businesses, which may lack the resources to hire dedicated financial analysts. By utilizing AI-powered financial tools, they can access sophisticated analytics typically reserved for larger enterprises.

One compelling example of AI in financial decision-making is the use of robo-advisors. Robo-advisors are automated platforms that provide financial advice and portfolio management services using algorithms and machine learning. They analyze clients' financial goals, risk tolerance, and investment preferences to create and manage personalized investment portfolios. This technology democratizes access to high-quality financial advice, making it available to a broader audience at a fraction of the cost of traditional financial advisors. By leveraging AI, individuals and businesses can make informed investment decisions, optimize their portfolios, and achieve their financial objectives.

Marketing is another domain where AI is providing a significant edge to businesses of all sizes. AI-driven marketing tools can analyze customer data, segment audiences, and predict consumer behavior with remarkable accuracy. This enables businesses to create highly targeted marketing campaigns, personalize customer interactions, and improve conversion rates. For example, AI algorithms can analyze past purchase history, browsing behavior, and demographic information to recommend products and services tailored to individual preferences. This level of personalization enhances customer satisfaction and loyalty, driving business growth.

In digital marketing, AI-powered tools like chatbots, predictive analytics, and recommendation engines have become indispensable. Chatbots use natural language processing (NLP) to engage with customers, answer queries, and provide personalized recommendations in real-time. Predictive analytics can forecast customer behavior, helping businesses optimize their marketing strategies and allocate resources more effectively. Recommendation engines, used by e-commerce giants like Amazon and Netflix, analyze customer data to suggest products and content that users are likely to enjoy, increasing engagement and sales.

Additionally, AI is transforming the way businesses conduct market research and competitive analysis. Traditional market research methods, such as surveys and focus groups, are often time-consuming and costly. In contrast, AI-driven tools can analyze vast amounts of online data, such as social media posts, customer reviews, and industry reports, to gain real-time insights into market trends and consumer sentiment. This allows businesses to respond swiftly to changing market dynamics, identify emerging opportunities, and stay ahead of the competition. For instance, sentiment analysis tools can gauge public perception of a brand or product by analyzing social media conversations, enabling businesses to adjust their marketing strategies accordingly.

Beyond finance and marketing, AI is enhancing decision-making processes in various other sectors. In supply chain management, AI-powered predictive analytics can forecast demand, optimize inventory levels, and streamline logistics operations. By analyzing historical sales data, supplier performance, and external factors such as weather and economic conditions, AI can predict future demand patterns and recommend optimal inventory levels. This helps businesses reduce stockouts, minimize excess inventory, and improve overall supply chain efficiency.

in healthcare, AI is revolutionizing patient care and clinical decision-making. Predictive models can analyze patient data to identify those at risk of developing chronic conditions, enabling early interventions and personalized treatment plans. AI-driven diagnostic tools assist healthcare professionals in making accurate diagnoses and recommending appropriate treatments. For example, AI algorithms can analyze medical images to detect anomalies, such as tumors or fractures, with a high degree of accuracy. This supports radiologists and other specialists in providing timely and accurate diagnoses.

AI is also playing a critical role in improving operational efficiency and reducing costs in various industries. In manufacturing, AI-powered predictive maintenance systems can monitor equipment performance and predict potential failures. By analyzing sensor data and machine logs, these systems can identify early warning signs of equipment malfunctions and recommend proactive maintenance measures. This reduces downtime, extends equipment lifespan, and minimizes repair costs.

Moreover, AI is enhancing decision-making in energy management and environmental sustainability. Predictive analytics can forecast energy demand, optimize the operation of renewable energy sources, and reduce energy consumption. For example, AI algorithms can predict electricity usage patterns and adjust the operation of power grids to balance supply and demand effectively. In agriculture, AI-driven tools can analyze weather data, soil conditions, and crop performance to recommend optimal planting and harvesting times, helping farmers improve productivity and reduce environmental impact.

The integration of artificial intelligence (AI) into decision-making processes offers substantial advantages, but it also presents significant ethical and legal challenges. To fully harness AI's potential while mitigating risks, it is essential to ensure fairness, transparency, and accountability in AI-driven decisions. Without these safeguards, biases and unintended consequences could arise, potentially undermining trust and equity. For instance, in the financial sector, AI models are increasingly used for tasks such as credit scoring and fraud detection. However, these systems must be rigorously tested to ensure they do not unintentionally discriminate against certain demographic groups or disadvantage specific customers due to hidden biases in the training data. Similarly, in the field of healthcare, predictive AI models are revolutionizing diagnostics, treatment recommendations, and resource allocation. Nonetheless, these systems must be carefully validated to ensure they provide accurate and equitable recommendations for all patients, regardless of their background or circumstances.

AI is fundamentally transforming the way decisions are made and predictive analytics are conducted across a wide range of industries. From finance and marketing to supply chain management and healthcare, organizations are leveraging AI to access advanced analytics, streamline operations, and gain a competitive edge in an increasingly data-driven global economy. For example, in marketing, AI helps businesses analyze consumer behavior to create personalized experiences, while in supply chain management, it optimizes inventory levels and forecasts demand with unprecedented accuracy.

The combination of AI and predictive analytics holds immense potential to enhance efficiency, reduce costs, and achieve superior outcomes. By automating routine tasks and providing insights that were previously unattainable, AI enables businesses to make more informed and timely decisions. However, the ethical implications of AI cannot be ignored. Addressing issues such as data privacy, algorithmic bias, and lack of transparency is critical to ensuring the responsible and sustainable use of AI technologies.

In conclusion, while AI offers transformative benefits in decision-making and predictive analytics, its implementation must be guided by a commitment to ethical principles. By prioritizing fairness, accountability, and transparency, organizations can maximize the advantages of AI while minimizing risks. This balanced approach will enable society to unlock AI's full potential, fostering innovation and progress in a way that benefits all stakeholders equitably.

CHAPTER 8 SUMMARY DIAGRAM:

Topic	Main Points
AI for Augmented Decision Making	AI has the remarkable capability to make informed decisions by processing vast amounts of data and identifying patterns.

	Humans can make much better decision when the size of data is small. One of the primary strengths of AI in decision-making is its objectivity, especially in healthcare. Some of the important things to consider during an AI model selection are objectives, constraints, and human collaboration.
Predictive Analytics and Its Applications	Statistical algorithms, historical data, and machine learning techniques, predictive analytics forecasts future events and trends in many disciplines including weather forecasting, healthcare, finance, etc.
Examples from Finance, Marketing, and Operations	Robo-advisors are automated platforms that provide financial advice and portfolio management services using algorithms and machine learning.

	in marketing, Chatbots provide customer service for FAQs and many other important jobs. Recommendation engines, used by e-commerce giants like Amazon and Netflix, analyze customer data to suggest products and content.

Knowledge Check:

Exercise "AI for Augmented Decision Making"

Question 1:

Which of the following is a primary strength of AI in decision-making?

A. It relies on human intuition to analyze small datasets.

B. It is influenced by emotions and external pressures.

C. It ensures decisions are based on data-driven evidence without biases.

D. It requires human input for repetitive tasks.

Question 2:

What is the first step in AI-augmented decision-making?

A. Data collection and preparation.

B. Model selection and training.

C. Problem definition and objective setting.

D. Monitoring and maintenance.

Exercise "Predictive Analytics and Its Applications"

Question 1:

How does AI enhance predictive analytics in weather forecasting?

A. By replacing historical data with real-time observations.

B. By identifying early warning signs of extreme weather events and improving prediction accuracy.

C. By allowing meteorologists to rely solely on AI without traditional weather models.

D. By eliminating the need for satellite imagery in weather prediction.

Question 2:

Which of the following is an ethical consideration associated with AI-driven predictive analytics?

A. Increasing computational costs for data processing.

B. Ensuring the privacy and integrity of customer data.

C. Reducing reliance on human decision-making in all scenarios.

D. Eliminating the need for domain knowledge in model development.

Question 1:

How do robo-advisors leverage AI to assist with financial decision-making?

A. By replacing traditional financial advisors entirely.

B. By analyzing financial goals, risk tolerance, and preferences to create personalized investment portfolios.

C. By predicting stock market crashes in real-time without historical data.

D. By offering financial advice without the use of machine learning or algorithms.

Question 2:

What is a significant ethical concern when implementing AI in predictive analytics?

A. The cost of developing AI models.

B. Ensuring fairness and preventing algorithmic bias in decision-making.

C. The inability of AI to process large datasets efficiently.

D. Lack of interest in AI from industry stakeholders.

CITATIONS:

1. Davenport, T., & Harris, J. (2017). Competing on Analytics: Updated, with a New Introduction: The New Science of Winning. Harvard Business Review Press.

2. Gentsch, P. (2019). AI in Marketing, Sales and Service: How Marketers Without a Data Science Degree Can Use AI, Big Data and Bots. Springer International Publishing.

REFERENCES:

Domingos, P. (2015). *The Master Algorithm: How the Quest for the Ultimate Learning Machine Will Remake Our World*. Basic Books.

Ransbotham, S., Kiron, D., Gerbert, P., & Reeves, M. (2017). Reshaping Business With Artificial Intelligence. *MIT Sloan Management Review*, 59(1), 1-17.

Topol, E. (2019). *Deep Medicine: How Artificial Intelligence Can Make Healthcare Human Again*. Basic Books.

Why Every Business Leader Needs to Understand AI

You don't have to be a tech wizard to make AI work for your business, just like you don't need to understand combustion engines to drive a car. But if you're a leader, your responsibility goes deeper than just using AI. You're the one deciding how it fits into your organization's goals, values, and vision. To do that, you need to grasp the fundamentals of how it operates.

This chapter dives into why today's business leaders need a basic understanding of AI. Whether it's about making informed decisions, maximizing your investment, or staying on the right side of legal and ethical lines, this knowledge is no longer optional. It's your competitive advantage.

AI as a Decision-Making Tool

Think of AI not as a silver bullet but as a sophisticated tool. Like any tool, its value depends on how you wield it. Choosing the right vendor, setting realistic expectations, and spotting areas where AI can genuinely add value are all skills rooted in understanding its basics.

For instance, recognizing that AI models rely heavily on the data they're trained on empowers you to ask critical questions. Is this tool trained on data relevant to your industry? Could it introduce biases or inaccuracies? When you understand these nuances, you're no longer at the mercy of the technology; you're steering it to serve your business.

Getting the Most Out of Your Investment

AI isn't a "set it and forget it" solution. It's more like a garden: it needs care, attention, and occasional weeding. Knowing how AI learns from data, improves through feedback, and delivers measurable outcomes allows you to fine-tune it for maximum impact.

Without this understanding, you're more likely to underutilize the tool—or worse, let it become a liability. A bit of knowledge can go a long way in ensuring that your investment in AI keeps paying dividends.

Managing Risks: Legal Compliance and Ethics

AI's power comes with risks, and ignoring them isn't an option. Legal and ethical challenges often lurk beneath the surface, and as a leader, it's on you to anticipate and mitigate them.

The data that feeds AI systems can be a legal minefield. Some tools are trained on datasets scraped from the internet—including copyrighted materials or private information used without consent. If your business adopts such a tool, you might unknowingly expose yourself to lawsuits.

To stay compliant, ask questions like:

- Where does the training data come from?
- Do we have the legal rights to use it?
- How does the tool adhere to privacy laws like GDPR or CCPA?

Being informed protects not just your bottom line but also your reputation as a conscientious leader.

ETHICS

AI doesn't operate in isolation. If it's trained on biased or unethical data, those flaws will show up in its decisions—and by extension, in your business operations. From AI-driven hiring tools that inadvertently favor certain demographics to chatbots generating offensive responses, the risks are real and often public.

The antidote? Oversight. Regularly review the training data, understand the tool's limitations, and monitor outputs for fairness and accuracy. Ensure your AI aligns with your organization's values—because when it comes to ethics, there's no room for autopilot.

Building Proprietary AI Tools

Off-the-shelf solutions might get you started, but creating custom AI models tailored to your business can set you apart. Imagine training a language model on your company's policy manuals, customer service logs, and product catalogs. These tools can deliver insights and efficiencies that generic AI simply can't match.

HOW THESE MODELS ARE TRAINED

Training involves feeding the model high-quality, relevant data so it can learn patterns and context. Garbage in, garbage out: if your data is outdated or inconsistent, so will be the results.

CONTINUOUS LEARNING

AI evolves based on the data and feedback it receives. It's not static, which means maintaining its accuracy and relevance requires regular updates and monitoring. Done right, this process transforms your AI into a long-term asset that grows with your business.

YOUR ROLE AS A LEADER

When you understand AI's mechanics, you're no longer just a user. You're the one shaping how it drives your organization forward. This knowledge enables you to:

- Collaborate effectively with AI developers.

- Identify and mitigate potential risks.
- Communicate clearly with your team about AI's benefits and limitations.
- Build trust with customers by demonstrating ethical AI use.

Your job isn't to master every technical detail—it's to lead with informed confidence.

The Big Picture: Driving Innovation and Growth

AI isn't just about cutting costs or automating repetitive tasks. It's a catalyst for innovation, enabling entirely new products, services, and business models. But to harness this potential, you need to go beyond buzzwords and understand what the technology can (and can't) do.

With this knowledge, you're equipped to:

- Dream bigger.
- Act smarter.
- Stay ahead in an AI-driven world.

Key Takeaways

- **Better Decision-Making:** Understanding AI helps you choose the right tools and ask the right questions.

- **Maximizing ROI:** Knowing how AI works ensures you get the most from your investment.
- **Managing Risks:** Awareness of legal and ethical issues protects your business and reputation.
- **Custom AI Models:** Tailored solutions provide a competitive edge.
- **Leadership:** Knowledge empowers you to drive innovation and inspire your team.

AI isn't the future—it's the present. By investing the time to understand it now, you're not just adapting. You're leading.

KNOWLEDGE CHECK

This section assesses your understanding of the ethical considerations, risk management, and leadership responsibilities associated with AI.

Questions:

1. What is one critical question to ask when adopting an AI tool to ensure legal compliance?
   a. How many developers worked on the tool?
   b. What is the source of its training data?
   c. Does it use open-source libraries?
   d. Can it operate without an internet connection?
2. True or False: AI tools are static and do not require regular updates once implemented.
3. Which of the following is NOT a potential ethical concern with AI?
   a. Biased decision-making

b. infringement of privacy laws
c. Lack of user-friendly interfaces
d. Unintended offensive outputs
4. How can businesses ensure fairness and accuracy in AI outputs?
a. By training AI on high-quality, unbiased data
b. By using the most expensive AI tools available
c. By automating oversight entirely
d. By relying solely on vendor assurances
5. Describe one way a business leader can demonstrate ethical AI use to build customer trust.

Exercise: Navigating Ethics and Risk in AI Adoption

Scenario:
You are a business leader tasked with implementing an AI-driven hiring tool. Based on this chapter, address the following:

1. Identify two critical questions to ask the vendor about the tool's training data and compliance with laws like GDPR or CCPA.
2. Propose one strategy to monitor and address potential biases in the tool's outputs.
3. Describe how you would communicate your ethical use of AI to employees and job candidates to build trust.

Objective: Apply concepts from this chapter to evaluate, mitigate risks, and align AI implementation with ethical standards.

REFERENCES

- General Data Protection Regulation (GDPR). (2016). *Official Journal of the European Union*. Retrieved from EU GDPR Information.
- California Consumer Privacy Act (CCPA). (2018). *State of California Department of Justice*. Retrieved from California DOJ CCPA Page.
- Binns, R. (2018). *Fairness in Machine Learning: Lessons from Political Philosophy. Proceedings of the 2020 Conference on Fairness, Accountability, and Transparency*. Retrieved from ACM Digital Library.
- OpenAI. (n.d.). *Ethics and Bias in AI Development*. Retrieved from OpenAI Blog.
- IBM Watson. (n.d.). *AI Governance and Ethics Framework*. Retrieved from IBM Watson.
- Jameson, G. (2024). *Ethical AI: A Guide to Responsible and Impactful Use*. WebStores Ltd.
- European Commission. (2024). *Overview of the AI Act*. Retrieved from EU AI Act.
- AI Now Institute. (n.d.). *Bias and Ethics in AI*. Retrieved from AI Now Institute.
- Partnership on AI. (n.d.). *Responsible AI Practices*. Retrieved from Partnership on AI.

CHAPTER 10: AI LIMITATIONS

Technical Constraints (Explainability, Scalability):

AI models have increasingly become central to daily life, aiding individuals from various professions in decision-making and task automation. These advanced tools can sift through immense data sets, detect patterns, and generate insights that would otherwise be impossible for humans to discern manually (Mueller & Massaron, 2021). Despite their convenience, these tools pose a major challenge in terms of transparency and trustworthiness.

Most users lack a detailed understanding of how AI systems generate their outputs, raising questions such as: What data is used? Which model processes this data? These uncertainties create significant transparency issues. For example, an AI tool might suggest a particular financial investment, but if users are unaware of the underlying data or the decision-making process, they might hesitate to trust the recommendation (Holzinger et al., 2017). Transparency is critical because it enables users to grasp the reasoning behind AI suggestions, thereby fostering trust and promoting informed decisions.

The reliability of AI-generated outcomes is another major concern. Many users do not have the technical expertise to verify the outputs from these tools. Consider a healthcare application that uses AI to provide potential diagnoses based on patient symptoms. Although the AI might analyze thousands of medical records to arrive at its suggestion, a user without medical knowledge could find it challenging to assess the accuracy of these diagnoses. Without validation from a subject matter expert, the reliability of AI-generated results remains questionable (Dalenberg et al., 2021).

To address these issues, it is essential that AI tools include explanations of how they derive their responses. Known as "explainability," this feature allows users to comprehend the steps and logic involved in the AI's decision-making process (Burkart & Huber, 2021). For instance, an explainable AI model in finance might list the factors considered during investment recommendations, such as market trends, historical data, and risk assessments. This transparency gives users critical insights and confidence in the tool's reliability.

Explainability also improves system accountability by making it easier to spot and rectify potential biases or errors. For instance, if an AI model used in hiring decisions disproportionately favors certain candidates, an explainable system can help pinpoint these biases and suggest corrections to ensure fairness and inclusivity.

Furthermore, subject matter experts play a vital role in verifying and interpreting AI results. These experts possess the knowledge and experience necessary to critically evaluate AI outputs. In fields such as healthcare, finance, and law, professionals' expertise ensures that AI recommendations are accurate, ethical, and aligned with industry standards (Madhavan et al., 2018). For instance, a doctor can verify an AI-generated diagnosis and provide additional context or insights the AI might have missed. Similarly, a financial advisor can assess AI-driven investment suggestions to ensure they fit a client's specific goals and risk tolerance.

Incorporating transparency and explainability in AI tools benefits users, developers, and stakeholders alike. For developers, understanding their AI models' workings allows them to continuously refine and improve their algorithms. Feedback from users and experts about the explanations' clarity and accuracy can drive innovation and lead to more robust AI solutions.

Moreover, transparency in AI cultivates greater public trust and acceptance of these technologies. When people understand how AI tools function, they are more likely to adopt and rely on them in their daily lives. This trust is particularly crucial in fields where AI's impact can be significant, such as healthcare, finance, and education. For instance, transparent AI applications in education can help educators identify students' learning needs and provide tailored interventions, resulting in better educational outcomes (Kuhlmann et al., 2021).

In conclusion, the widespread use of AI tools across various domains underscores the importance of transparency and reliability. To build trust and ensure the ethical use of AI, it is essential to implement explainability features that allow users to understand how these tools derive their results (Xu & Ramesh, 2019). Subject matter experts also play a crucial role in verifying AI outputs, ensuring their accuracy and reliability (Guidotti et al., 2019). By prioritizing transparency and explainability, we can foster greater trust and acceptance of AI technologies, leading to more informed and confident use of these powerful tools.

Artificial Intelligence (AI) has revolutionized various industries by automating tasks, optimizing processes, and providing deep insights through data analysis. However, the efficiency and effectiveness of AI systems heavily depend on the underlying hardware and algorithms. Among the critical hardware components used in AI is the Graphics Processing Unit (GPU), which has significantly contributed to the advancement of machine learning and deep learning technologies. Nonetheless, as the volume of data continues to grow exponentially, the need for sophisticated hardware and efficient algorithms becomes increasingly paramount.

GPUs are designed to handle massive parallel processing tasks, making them ideal for training AI models. Unlike traditional Central Processing Units (CPUs), which excel at sequential processing, GPUs can perform many computations simultaneously, drastically reducing the time required for training complex AI models. This capability is particularly important for deep learning, which involves training models with multiple layers of neurons and a vast number of parameters. For instance, cutting-edge applications such as natural language processing (NLP) and computer vision rely on GPUs to process and analyze large datasets efficiently.

However, the continuous growth of data presents significant challenges. As AI models become more sophisticated and the datasets, they process become larger, the demand for high-performance hardware intensifies. This increase in demand necessitates not only more powerful GPUs but also other advanced hardware components, such as Tensor Processing Units (TPUs) and specialized AI accelerators. These components are designed to optimize specific tasks within AI workflows, further enhancing the speed and efficiency of model training and inference.

The increasing complexity of AI models and the growing volume of data also put a strain on traditional data storage and memory solutions. For AI systems to operate effectively, they require fast access to massive amounts of data, leading to the development of advanced storage solutions such as Non-Volatile Memory Express (NVMe) drives and high-bandwidth memory (HBM). These technologies ensure that data can be quickly loaded into GPUs for processing, minimizing bottlenecks and improving overall system performance.

However, the pursuit of faster hardware and state-of-the-art algorithms comes with significant costs. High-performance GPUs, TPUs, and other specialized hardware are expensive, making it challenging for smaller organizations and researchers with limited budgets to access these resources. This cost barrier creates a divide between entities that can afford cutting-edge technology and those that cannot, potentially widening the gap in AI development and adoption.

Additionally, the power consumption of high-performance hardware is a critical consideration. GPUs and other advanced components require substantial energy, leading to increased operational costs and environmental impact. As AI continues to evolve, finding ways to improve the energy efficiency of these systems is crucial. Researchers are exploring innovative cooling solutions, energy-efficient architectures, and optimization techniques to mitigate the power consumption of AI hardware.

Meeting the growing demands of AI requires not only faster hardware but also state-of-the-art algorithms. As AI models become more complex, developing efficient algorithms that can leverage the capabilities of advanced hardware is essential. These algorithms must be designed to handle large datasets, optimize performance, and provide accurate results. Innovations in algorithm design, such as distributed computing and federated learning, aim to improve the scalability and efficiency of AI systems while maintaining data privacy and security.

Distributed computing involves dividing a large computational task into smaller, manageable sub-tasks that can be processed simultaneously across multiple machines. This approach leverages the power of multiple GPUs, CPUs, or other hardware components, significantly reducing training times for large AI models. Federated learning, on the other hand, enables AI models to be trained across decentralized devices or servers without sharing raw data. This technique not only enhances data privacy but also reduces the need for massive data transfers, alleviating some of the strain on hardware resources.

The rapid pace of AI development means that research must continually keep up with advancements in hardware and software. Researchers and engineers must stay abreast of the latest technological innovations to ensure that AI systems remain efficient and effective. This continuous cycle of innovation requires significant investments in research and development (R&D), as well as collaboration between academic institutions, industry leaders, and government agencies.

Furthermore, the integration of AI with emerging technologies such as quantum computing holds promise for overcoming current hardware limitations. Quantum computing has the potential to perform calculations at speeds unimaginable with classical computers, potentially revolutionizing AI, and other fields. While quantum computing is still in its early stages, ongoing research is exploring its applications in AI, such as optimizing complex algorithms and solving problems that are currently computationally infeasible.

In conclusion, the effectiveness of AI systems is inherently linked to the performance of the hardware and algorithms they rely on. As data volumes grow and AI models become hardware and efficient algorithms intensifies, posing significant technical and financial constraints. Continuous research and development are essential to keep up with advancements in both hardware and software, ensuring that AI remains a powerful and reliable tool across various domains. Collaboration, innovation, and investment in cutting-edge technologies are crucial to overcoming these challenges and realizing the full potential of AI.

Societal Limitations (Regulation, Acceptance):

The rapid expansion of artificial intelligence (AI) has garnered significant excitement and interest across various industries and facets of everyday life. The technology promises to revolutionize the way we live, work, and interact with the world around us. From self-driving cars and personalized healthcare to automated customer service and advanced data analytics, AI is becoming an integral part of modern society. However, alongside the myriad benefits, there are inherent limitations and concerns that need to be addressed to ensure the responsible and ethical development and deployment of AI systems.

One of the primary concerns regarding AI is the lack of comprehensive regulations governing its use. Currently, the regulatory landscape for AI is fragmented and inconsistent across different countries and industries. This lack of standardized guidelines creates a sense of uncertainty and hesitation among the public and various stakeholders. People are still coming to terms with the idea that AI is becoming an everyday reality, and this transition is accompanied by a range of emotional and psychological responses, from excitement to fear and skepticism.

The excitement surrounding AI is understandable, given its potential to solve complex problems and enhance human capabilities. For instance, AI-driven medical diagnostics can identify diseases at an early stage, potentially saving lives and reducing healthcare costs. In the financial sector, AI algorithms can detect fraudulent activities with greater accuracy and speed than traditional methods. Additionally, AI-powered educational tools can provide personalized learning experiences, catering to the unique needs of individual students. These advancements highlight the transformative power of AI and its ability to create positive change in society.

However, the flip side of this excitement is the concern about the ethical implications and potential misuse of AI. One of the fundamental limitations of AI is its reliance on data. AI systems are only as good as the data they are trained on, and biased or incomplete data can lead to flawed outcomes. This raises questions about fairness, accountability, and transparency in AI decision-making processes. For example, if an AI system used for hiring decisions is trained on biased data, it may perpetuate existing inequalities and discrimination in the workplace.

Moreover, the issue of control and oversight is paramount. Who is responsible for the actions and decisions made by AI systems? In cases where AI systems cause harm or make erroneous decisions, determining liability can be challenging. This lack of clear accountability can erode trust in AI technologies and hinder their widespread adoption. Ensuring that AI systems are transparent and explainable is crucial to building trust and confidence among users.

Another critical concern is the potential for AI to be used for unethical purposes. As with any powerful technology, there are individuals and organizations that may seek to exploit AI for malicious reasons. For instance, AI-generated deepfakes can be used to spread misinformation and manipulate public opinion. Autonomous weapons powered by AI pose significant risks to global security and raise ethical dilemmas about the use of lethal force. The potential for AI to be weaponized highlights the urgent need for robust regulations and international cooperation to prevent its misuse.

The impact of AI on the workforce is another area of concern. While AI has the potential to create new job opportunities and enhance productivity, it also threatens to displace a significant number of jobs. Automation of routine tasks and processes can lead to job losses in industries such as manufacturing, retail, and transportation. This transition requires careful management to ensure that workers are not left behind and that there are adequate measures in place to support retraining and reskilling initiatives.

Furthermore, the long-term implications of AI on human well-being and society cannot be overlooked. There is an ongoing debate about the "end game" of AI and what the future holds. Will AI ultimately benefit humanity, or will it pose existential risks? Prominent voices in the tech industry, such as Elon Musk and Stephen Hawking, have warned about the potential dangers of AI, including the possibility of creating superintelligent systems that may act in ways that are not aligned with human values and interests.

Addressing these concerns requires a multi-faceted approach that involves collaboration between governments, industry leaders, researchers, and civil society. Establishing comprehensive and adaptive regulatory frameworks is essential to ensure the safe and ethical development of AI technologies. Policymakers must consider the diverse and evolving nature of AI applications and work towards creating regulations that are flexible and forward-looking.

In addition to regulations, fostering a culture of responsible AI development is crucial. This includes promoting ethical principles such as fairness, transparency, and accountability in AI research and deployment. Organizations must prioritize the ethical implications of their AI projects and actively work to mitigate potential biases and risks. Engaging diverse stakeholders in the AI development process can help identify and address ethical challenges from multiple perspectives.

Education and public awareness also play a vital role in shaping the future of AI. Increasing digital literacy and understanding of AI technologies can empower individuals to make informed decisions and participate in discussions about the ethical and societal implications of AI. Encouraging interdisciplinary research that brings together experts from fields such as computer science, ethics, law, and social sciences can provide a holistic understanding of the challenges and opportunities presented by AI.

In conclusion, while the advancements in AI technology are undoubtedly exciting and hold great promise, it is essential to address the limitations and concerns associated with its development and deployment. Comprehensive regulations, ethical considerations, and public awareness are key to ensuring that AI serves the best interests of humanity. By adopting a proactive and collaborative approach, we can harness the full potential of AI while safeguarding against its risks and ensuring a positive impact on society.

Two School of Thoughts:

The rising prominence of AI and its applications has created two prominent camps with opposing viewpoints. The first camp perceives AI as a remarkable opportunity brimming with potential for innovation and progress. Enthusiastic to exploit AI's capabilities, this group aims to boost productivity, efficiency, and overall quality of life. They foresee AI revolutionizing sectors such as healthcare, finance, education, and entertainment. According to their vision, AI is the key to solving intricate problems, automating repetitive tasks, and unlocking new horizons previously thought unattainable.

For example, AI-driven medical diagnostics can lead to improved patient outcomes by enabling faster and more precise diagnoses, while AI-powered financial algorithms can optimize investment strategies and minimize risks. This optimistic group champions the broad adoption of AI technologies, anticipating the transformative benefits that AI can bring to society.

In stark contrast, the second camp adopts a more cautious and skeptical stance towards the rapid advancements in AI. This group is either hesitant to embrace such swift changes or is deeply concerned about the ethical and societal implications. They fear the potential misuse of AI, leading to negative consequences such as privacy infringements, job losses, and the erosion of human values. For instance, the misuse of AI in surveillance could infringe on individual privacy rights, while AI-driven automation could lead to significant job losses in certain sectors (Bostrom, 2014).

This group stresses the necessity for strict regulations and ethical guidelines to manage AI development and deployment responsibly. They argue that without proper oversight, AI could exacerbate existing inequalities and introduce new ethical dilemmas. The concerns raised by this group emphasize the importance of ensuring AI is developed and used responsibly, with a focus on preserving human values and societal well-being (Future of Life Institute, 2020).

Topics	Positive	Negative
Technical Constraints (Explainability, Scalability)	AI models have increasingly become central to daily life, aiding individuals from various professions in decision-making and task automation. These advanced tools can sift through immense data sets, detect patterns, and generate insights. For small dataset,	Difficult for a human to analyze large dataset. Most AI systems do not provide explanation how the results were obtained. Most AI systems do not do well when the dataset is small.

	humans expertise is more useful. For large datasets, sophisticated hardware like GPUs and TPUs are used along with Quantum Computing.	
Societal Limitations (Regulation, Acceptance)	Rapid expansion of artificial intelligence (AI) has garnered significant excitement and interest across various industries and	Most AI systems lack clear regulations and guidelines for implementation and oversight. Additionally, there is hesitation among people to adopt the latest AI tools, possibly due

	facets of everyday life.	to a lack of trust in AI-generated results across various domains and concerns about ethical implications.
Two School of Thoughts	One school of thought is that AI and the latest trends are the source of enormous opportunity.	There are fears that AI could lead to job displacement and potentially compromise ethical standards.

Knowledge Check:

Exercise on "Technical Constraints (Explainability, Scalability)":

1. What is one of the primary challenges users face with AI systems, as discussed in the passage?

A. Lack of computing hardware

B. Lack of transparency and trustworthiness

C. Over-reliance on explainability features

D. Insufficient data for decision-making

2. Why are GPUs considered essential for AI model training?

A. They are cost-effective for small organizations.

B. They excel at sequential processing tasks.

C. They handle massive parallel processing efficiently.

D. They have higher energy efficiency than TPUs.

Exercise on "Societal Limitations (Regulation, Acceptance)":

1.What is one of the major ethical concerns associated with AI, as discussed in the passage?

A. AI systems cannot solve complex problems.

B. AI systems may perpetuate biases if trained on flawed data.

C. AI systems require minimal oversight or control.

D. AI systems are too expensive to implement.

2.What is a suggested way to ensure the responsible development and deployment of AI technologies?

A. Limit AI applications to non-critical fields.

B. Establish comprehensive and adaptive regulatory frameworks.

C. Focus solely on technical advancements without ethical considerations.

D. Avoid collaboration between governments and private organizations.

Exercise on "Two School of Thoughts":

1.What is the primary concern of the group that takes a cautious stance toward AI?

A. AI's inability to improve healthcare and finance.

B. The potential misuse of AI, leading to privacy violations and job losses.

C. AI's inefficiency in solving intricate problems.

D. Lack of interest in automating repetitive tasks.

2.What is one of the benefits highlighted by the optimistic group regarding AI's impact on society?

A. AI will eliminate the need for ethical oversight.

B. AI will reduce the complexity of regulations in technology.

C. AI can improve patient outcomes through faster and

more accurate medical diagnostics.

D. AI can replace human values with automated decision-making processes.

REFERENCES:

1. Bostrom, N. (2014). Superintelligence: Paths, Dangers, Strategies. Oxford University Press.

2. Burkart, N., & Huber, M. F. (2021). A survey on the explainability of supervised machine learning. *Journal of Artificial Intelligence Research, 70*, 245-317. https://doi.org/10.1613/jair.1.12228

3. Dean, J., & Ghemawat, S. (2008). MapReduce: Simplified data processing on large clusters. *Communications of the ACM, 51*(1), 107-113. https://doi.org/10.1145/1327452.1327492

4. Future of Life Institute. (2020). AI Policy - Global. Retrieved from https://futureoflife.org/ai-policy-global/

5. Kuhlmann, M., Farmer, W., & Bishop, C. M. (2021). Transparency and generalization in AI-intensive domains: A review of the role of explainability. In

Advances in Neural Information Processing Systems (Vol. 33, pp. 4521-4533).

6. McAfee, A., & Brynjolfsson, E. (2017). Machine, platform, crowd: Harnessing our digital future. *W. W. Norton & Company.*

Diagnostic AI Systems and Personalized Medicine:

AI systems are revolutionizing the healthcare industry, providing substantial assistance to physicians, pharmacists, and health scientists in diagnosing patients. These intelligent systems can analyze vast amounts of data, including medical records, lab results, and imaging studies, to identify patterns and make predictions that can aid in diagnosis. By leveraging historical data, AI can also assist in making informed decisions in personalized medicine, ensuring that treatment plans are tailored to the individual patient's needs and circumstances.

One of the significant advantages of AI in healthcare is its ability to reduce errors. The decisions made by AI systems are less error-prone because they rely on extensive data analysis and evidence-based algorithms. This can lead to more accurate diagnoses and treatment plans, ultimately improving patient outcomes. For example, AI algorithms can analyze imaging studies such as X-rays, MRIs, and CT scans with a high degree of accuracy, often detecting abnormalities that may be missed by human eyes. This can

185

be particularly valuable in early detection of diseases such as cancer, where timely intervention can make a significant difference in prognosis.

In the field of surgery, robots are already making a considerable impact. Robotic-assisted surgery allows for greater precision and control, reducing the risk of complications and improving recovery times. These robots can be programmed to perform specific tasks with a high degree of accuracy, making complex surgeries less invasive and more efficient. Surgeons can use robotic systems to operate on patients with more precision, leading to better outcomes and shorter hospital stays. Additionally, these systems can be equipped with AI algorithms that assist surgeons in real-time, providing valuable insights and recommendations based on the patient's data.

The AI software used in healthcare can be trained from the expertise of many human experts in the field. This involves feeding the AI system with vast amounts of data, including medical literature, clinical guidelines, and real-world patient data. As the AI system learns from this information, it becomes more adept at identifying patterns and making predictions. This training process enables the

AI to assist physicians at all levels of experience, from medical students to seasoned practitioners. For example, an AI-powered decision support system can provide junior doctors with evidence-based recommendations, helping them make more informed decisions in their clinical practice.

AI systems also have the potential to enhance the efficiency of healthcare delivery. By automating routine tasks such as appointment scheduling, billing, and inventory management, AI can free up healthcare professionals to focus on patient care. Additionally, AI-powered chatbots and virtual assistants can provide patients with 24/7 access to healthcare information and support, improving patient engagement and satisfaction. For instance, a virtual assistant can answer common health questions, provide medication reminders, and even help patients navigate their treatment plans.

The integration of AI in healthcare is not without challenges. There are concerns related to data privacy and security, as the use of AI requires access to sensitive patient information. Ensuring that this data is protected and used ethically is paramount. Additionally, there is a need for ongoing training and education for healthcare professionals to ensure they can effectively use AI tools in their practice. As AI technology continues to evolve, it will be essential to establish robust regulatory frameworks to ensure its safe and effective use in healthcare.

Despite these challenges, the potential benefits of AI in healthcare are immense. AI has the power to transform how healthcare is delivered, making it more accurate, efficient, and personalized. By harnessing the capabilities of AI, healthcare providers can improve patient outcomes, reduce costs, and enhance the overall quality of care. As AI technology continues to advance, its role in healthcare is likely to expand, offering new and innovative solutions to some of the industry's most pressing challenges.

In conclusion, AI systems offer numerous benefits to physicians, pharmacists, and health scientists in diagnosing patients and making informed decisions in personalized medicine. With their ability to analyze vast amounts of data and reduce errors, AI systems can significantly improve patient outcomes. The use of robots in surgery and the training of AI software from human experts further highlight the transformative potential of AI in healthcare. As the industry continues to embrace AI, it will be essential to address the associated challenges to ensure that this technology can be used effectively and ethically.

AI for Drug Discovery and Medical Research:

AI has revolutionized numerous industries, and its impact on healthcare, particularly in the realms of drug discovery and medical research, is especially profound. One of the key advantages of AI is its ability to manage and analyze vast amounts of data efficiently, providing insights that would be nearly impossible for humans to uncover alone. This capability is especially significant in drug discovery and medical research, where the volume of data can be immense and complex.

In the field of drug discovery, the process of developing a new drug is notoriously time-consuming and expensive. Traditional methods often involve a trial-and-error approach, where researchers screen thousands of compounds to identify potential drug candidates. This process can take years and cost billions of dollars. AI can significantly streamline this process by analyzing large datasets to identify patterns and predict the efficacy of potential drug candidates. Machine learning algorithms can sift through vast amounts of data from clinical trials, scientific literature, and genomic studies to identify promising compounds more quickly and accurately.

For instance, AI can analyze genetic data to identify specific biomarkers associated with a disease, allowing researchers to develop targeted therapies. This approach, known as precision medicine, aims to tailor treatments to individual patients based on their genetic makeup. By leveraging AI, researchers can analyze the genetic profiles of large populations to identify commonalities and differences that may influence how patients respond to treatments. This can lead to the development of more effective and personalized therapies, ultimately improving patient outcomes.

In addition to identifying potential drug candidates, AI can also predict how these compounds will interact with the human body. This is achieved through the analysis of biological data and the simulation of drug interactions at the molecular level. By predicting the pharmacokinetics and pharmacodynamics of a drug, AI can help researchers understand how it will be absorbed, distributed, metabolized, and excreted by the body. This information is crucial for determining the optimal dosage and minimizing potential side effects, thereby improving the safety and efficacy of new drugs.

Medical research also benefits significantly from the application of AI, particularly when it comes to managing large datasets. Researchers often need to analyze vast amounts of data from diverse sources, such as electronic health records (EHRs), medical imaging, and genomic studies. The sheer volume and complexity of this data can be overwhelming, making it challenging for researchers to extract meaningful insights. AI can help by automating the process of data analysis, identifying patterns and correlations that may not be immediately apparent to human researchers.

One powerful AI technique used in medical research is unsupervised learning, which involves training algorithms to identify patterns in data without predefined labels. This approach is particularly useful for clustering data based on similarities, which can help researchers identify subgroups within a population that share common characteristics. For example, unsupervised learning algorithms can analyze genetic data to identify clusters of patients with similar genetic mutations, which may be associated with specific diseases or responses to treatment. Once these clusters are identified, researchers can work with subject matter experts to draw meaningful health conclusions and develop targeted interventions.

Moreover, AI can assist in the interpretation of complex medical data. For example, machine learning algorithms can analyze medical images, such as X-rays, MRIs, and CT scans, to detect abnormalities and diagnose diseases. These algorithms can identify patterns in the images that may be indicative of certain conditions, such as tumors or fractures, with a high degree of accuracy. By automating the process of image analysis, AI can help radiologists and other healthcare professionals diagnose diseases more quickly and accurately, leading to earlier interventions and better patient outcomes.

AI can also enhance the efficiency of clinical trials, which are a critical component of medical research. Traditional clinical trials often involve manually collecting and analyzing data from participants, which can be time-consuming and prone to errors. AI can streamline this process by automating data collection and analysis, ensuring that data is accurate and consistent. For example, AI-powered platforms can monitor patients remotely, collecting data on their vital signs, symptoms, and medication adherence in real-time. This data can then be analyzed to identify trends and assess the efficacy of the intervention.

Furthermore, AI can help researchers design more effective clinical trials by identifying the most suitable participants. By analyzing large datasets, AI can identify patients who meet the specific criteria for a trial, such as those with a particular genetic profile or disease progression. This can help ensure that the trial is conducted with a representative sample of the population, leading to more reliable and generalizable results. Additionally, AI can predict potential outcomes and identify any potential risks associated with the trial, allowing researchers to make informed decisions and minimize potential issues.

The integration of AI in healthcare data management and analysis also raises important ethical and regulatory considerations. Ensuring the privacy and security of patient data is paramount, as AI systems often require access to sensitive information. Healthcare organizations must implement robust data protection measures to safeguard patient information and comply with relevant regulations, such as the Health Insurance Portability and Accountability Act (HIPAA) in the United States. Additionally, it is essential to ensure that AI algorithms are transparent and explainable, allowing researchers and healthcare professionals to understand how decisions are being made.

In conclusion, AI has the potential to revolutionize drug discovery and medical research by efficiently managing and analyzing large datasets. By leveraging AI techniques such as unsupervised learning, researchers can cluster data based on similarities and draw meaningful health conclusions. AI can also streamline the drug discovery process, predict drug interactions, and enhance the efficiency of clinical trials. However, it is crucial to address ethical and regulatory considerations to ensure the responsible use of AI in healthcare. As AI technology continues to advance, its role in healthcare data management and analysis is likely to expand, offering new advancing medical research.

Ethical Implications in Medical AI:

The integration of artificial intelligence (AI) in healthcare has brought about significant advancements, but it also raises profound ethical implications, particularly regarding access to patients' data. One of the main ethical concerns is ensuring that patients are fully informed about how their health-related data will be used. Transparent communication is essential to maintain trust between patients and healthcare providers. Patients should be made aware that their data may be utilized for medical research purposes, with the goal of improving healthcare outcomes for all.

Informed consent is a cornerstone of ethical medical practice. Patients have the right to know what data is being collected, how it will be used, and who will have access to it. This ensures that patients can make informed decisions about their participation in research and data sharing. In the context of AI, informed consent becomes even more critical because the data used can be extensive and multifaceted, including electronic health records (EHRs), genomic data, imaging studies, and more.

To address this, healthcare providers must develop clear and comprehensible consent forms that explain the purposes and potential benefits of AI-driven research. These forms should also outline the risks, including potential privacy concerns and the measures taken to mitigate them. For example, data anonymization techniques can be employed to protect patients' identities. Anonymization involves removing or altering personal identifiers, such as names and social security numbers, so that the data cannot be traced back to specific individuals.

Despite the use of anonymization, there is always a risk of re-identification, especially when dealing with large datasets and advanced data analysis techniques. Therefore, robust data security measures must be implemented to safeguard patient information. This includes encryption, access controls, and regular audits to detect and prevent unauthorized access. Ensuring data security is not only an ethical obligation but also a legal requirement under regulations such as the Health insurance Portability and Accountability Act (HIPAA) in the United States.

Another ethical implication of AI in healthcare is the potential for bias in AI algorithms. AI systems are trained on historical data, and if this data contains biases, the AI's decisions may also be biased. For example, if an AI system is trained on data from a predominantly white population, it may not perform as well when applied to patients of other ethnicities. This can lead to disparities in healthcare outcomes. To mitigate this, it is essential to ensure that the training data is representative of the diverse patient population. Additionally, regular audits of AI systems should be conducted to identify and address any biases.

The primary purpose of AI data analysis in healthcare should be to obtain useful insights in fighting similar diseases. AI can identify patterns and correlations in data that may not be apparent to human researchers, leading to new discoveries and treatment options. For example, AI can analyze genetic data to identify biomarkers associated with specific diseases, which can then be used to develop targeted therapies. This can significantly improve the effectiveness of treatments and reduce adverse effects.

However, the use of AI in healthcare also requires careful consideration of the implications for patient autonomy. Patients must be informed about the role of AI in their care and the potential benefits and risks. For example, if a robot-assisted surgery is being considered, the patient should be informed about the technology, how it works, and the potential advantages and disadvantages. Informed consent must be obtained before any procedure is performed, ensuring that patients could ask questions and make informed decisions about their care.

In the case of robot-assisted surgeries, it is essential to communicate the potential benefits, such as increased precision and reduced recovery times, as well as the risks, such as technical failures or lack of human intuition. Patients should also be informed about the extent of human involvement in the procedure. For example, while robots can perform certain tasks with high precision, a human surgeon is still responsible for overseeing the procedure and making critical decisions.

The ethical implications of AI in healthcare extend beyond patient consent and data security. There are also concerns related to the accountability and transparency of AI systems. For example, if an AI system makes an incorrect diagnosis or recommendation, who is responsible? Ensuring that AI systems are transparent and explainable is crucial for maintaining trust and accountability. Healthcare providers must be able to understand and explain how AI systems arrive at their decisions, and mechanisms must be in place to address errors and rectify them.

Moreover, the use of AI in healthcare must be guided by ethical principles such as beneficence, non-maleficence, and justice. Beneficence involves ensuring that AI systems are designed and used to promote the well-being of patients. Non-maleficence requires that AI systems do not cause harm, and justice involves ensuring that the benefits and risks of AI are distributed fairly across all patient populations.

To uphold these principles, it is essential to involve a diverse range of stakeholders in the development and implementation of AI systems in healthcare. This includes not only healthcare providers and researchers but also patients, ethicists, and policymakers. Engaging patients in the design and implementation of AI systems can help ensure that their values and preferences are considered.

Ethicists can provide guidance on ethical considerations, while policymakers can establish regulations and guidelines to ensure the responsible use of AI in healthcare.

In conclusion, the integration of AI in healthcare presents significant ethical implications, particularly regarding access to patients' data. Ensuring informed consent, protecting patient privacy, and addressing potential biases are critical to maintaining trust and promoting the ethical use of AI. The primary purpose of AI data analysis should be to obtain useful insights in fighting similar diseases, and any procedure involving AI or robots must be performed with the patient's consent. By upholding ethical principles and involving diverse stakeholders, we can harness the potential of AI to improve healthcare outcomes while respecting patients' rights and autonomy.

A Final Note for the Medical Community:

The medical community stands to gain significantly from the integration of artificial intelligence (AI) technology. One of the key areas of potential is the complex data analysis of vast databases, including statewide patient databases, national Medicare databases, and specialized databases established by societies such as the Society of Thoracic Surgeons (STS), the American Association for Thoracic Surgery (AATS), the National Surgical Quality Improvement Program (NSQIP) database, and the United Network for Organ Sharing (UNOS) database. The capacity of AI to develop algorithms for the interpretation of CAT scans and X-rays further highlights its potential in revolutionizing medical practice. The authors feel very passionate to help the medical community in this regard.

The process of data analysis in the medical field involves several critical steps to ensure accurate and meaningful insights. Here is a step-by-step process for data analysis:

1. **Data Collection**: The first step involves gathering data from various sources such as electronic health records (EHRs), patient registries, clinical trials, and other relevant databases. This data can be obtained from statewide patient databases, national Medicare databases, and specialized databases established by medical societies.

2. **Data Cleaning**: Once the data is collected, it needs to be cleaned to remove any inconsistencies,

errors, or missing values. This step is crucial to ensure the accuracy and reliability of the analysis.

3. **Data Integration**: In this step, data from different sources is integrated to create a comprehensive dataset. This involves merging datasets, resolving any discrepancies, and ensuring that the data is in a uniform format.

4. **Data Exploration and Visualization**: Before diving into the analysis, it is important to explore and visualize the data to gain a better understanding of its structure and identify any patterns or trends. This can be done using various data visualization tools and techniques.

5. **Feature Engineering**: Feature engineering involves selecting and transforming the relevant features or variables from the dataset that will be used in the analysis. This step is essential for improving the performance of the AI model.

6. **Model Selection and Training**: The next step involves selecting an appropriate AI model for the analysis and training it on the dataset. This involves

dividing the data into training and testing sets, tuning the model parameters, and evaluating its performance.

7. **Model Evaluation and Validation**: Once the model is trained, it needs to be evaluated and validated to ensure its accuracy and reliability. This can be done using various evaluation metrics such as accuracy, precision, recall, and F1 score.

8. **Interpretation and Reporting**: The final step involves interpreting the results of the analysis and reporting the findings. This involves generating insights, identifying key predictors, and making recommendations for clinical practice or further research.

A subject matter expert (SME) will be needed throughout the process, especially during step 7 and 8. One possible AI model that can be used for medical data analysis is the Random Forest algorithm. Random Forest is an ensemble learning method that combines multiple decision trees to improve the accuracy and robustness of the predictions. It is particularly well-suited for handling large and complex datasets, making it an ideal choice for medical data analysis. The model can be used to develop predictors for surgical outcomes, complications, mortality, and morbidity, as well as to identify important features and relationships within the data.

The benefits of AI in medicine extend beyond data analysis. AI can also be a powerful tool for clinical outcomes research, administrative and business improvements in medical practice, and enhancing the overall quality of patient care. By leveraging AI, healthcare professionals can gain valuable insights, make informed decisions, and ultimately improve patient outcomes.

CHAPTER 11 SUMMARY DIAGRAM:

Topics	Positive	Negative
Diagnostic AI Systems and Personalized Medicine	Enhanced Accuracy and Precision Improved Efficiency	Data Privacy and Security Concerns Need for Ongoing Training
Ethical Implications in Medical AI	Enhanced Patient Outcomes	Risk of Data Re-identification Potential for Bias in AI Algorithms

	informed Consent and Transparency	
A Final Note for the Medical Community	Advanced Data Analysis Enhanced Clinical Outcomes	Data Privacy Concerns Dependence on Subject Matter Experts

Knowledge Check:

Exercise on "Diagnostic AI Systems and Personalized Medicine":

What is one of the significant advantages of AI in healthcare?

a) AI systems are more prone to errors

b) AI systems can make personalized treatment plans less effective

c) AI systems can assist in early detection of diseases like cancer

d) AI systems are unable to analyze imaging studies

How can AI enhance the efficiency of healthcare delivery?

a) By automating routine tasks such as appointment scheduling and billing

b) By making surgeries more invasive and complex

c) By providing patients with fewer access points to healthcare information

d) By reducing the need for ongoing training of healthcare professionals

Exercise on "Ethical Implications in Medical AI":

Question 1:

What is a key ethical concern regarding the use of AI in healthcare?

a) The reduction in the number of healthcare professionals

b) Ensuring patients are fully informed about how their data will be used

c) The increased cost of healthcare services

d) The difficulty in accessing advanced AI technology

What measure can be taken to protect patients' identities in AI-driven research?

a) Storing data in physical files

b) Using data anonymization techniques

c) Limiting access to medical literature

d) Increasing the number of medical researchers

Exercise on "A Final Note for the Medical Community":

Question 1:

Which of the following is a key area of potential for AI in the medical field?

a) Data cleaning and organization

b) Complex data analysis of vast databases

c) Developing new pharmaceutical drugs

d) Managing hospital staff schedules

Question 2:

What is the primary purpose of using the Random Forest algorithm in medical data analysis?

a) To create electronic health records (EHRs)

b) To merge datasets from different sources

c) To develop predictors for surgical outcomes and identify important features

d) To visualize data patterns and trends

CITATIONS:

1. Esteva, A., Robicquet, A., Ramsundar, B., Kuleshov, V., DePristo, M., Chou, K., ... & Dean, J. (2019). A guide to deep learning in healthcare. *Nature Medicine*, 25(1), 24-29. https://doi.org/10.1038/s41591-018-0316-z

2. Floridi, L., & Taddeo, M. (2016). What is data ethics? *Philosophical Transactions of the Royal Society A: Mathematical, Physical and Engineering Sciences*, 374(2083), 20160360. https://doi.org/10.1098/rsta.2016.0360

5. Obermeyer, Z., & Emanuel, E. J. (2016). Predicting the Future—Big Data, Machine Learning, and Clinical Medicine. *New England Journal of Medicine*, 375(13), 1216-1219. https://doi.org/10.1056/NEJMp1606181

4. Rajkomar, A., Dean, J., & Kohane, I. (2019). Machine learning in medicine. The New England Journal of Medicine, 380(14), 1347-1358.

5. Topol, E. (2019). High-performance medicine: the convergence of human and artificial intelligence. *Nature Medicine*, 25(1), 44-56. https://doi.org/10.1038/s41591-018-0300-7

CHAPTER 1 : FUTURE OF AI AND MARKET TRENDS

As we stand at the cusp of unprecedented technological evolution, Artificial Intelligence (AI) continues to redefine the contours of society and the global economy. This chapter delves into the anticipated key AI trends over the next decade, examines AI's role in shaping societal and economic landscapes, and discusses strategies for preparing for an AI-driven future. Integral to this discussion are concepts such as Artificial General Intelligence (AGI), Artificial Superintelligence (ASI), AI Agents and the recent disruptive impact of DeepSeek on AI predictions.

Key AI Trends in the Next Decade

1. EMERGENCE OF ARTIFICIAL GENERAL INTELLIGENCE (AGI):

AGI refers to machines capable of understanding, learning, and applying intelligence across a broad range of tasks, matching or surpassing human cognitive abilities. While current AI systems excel in narrow applications, the pursuit of AGI aims for more generalized capabilities.

Recent advancements suggest that AGI may be closer than previously anticipated, with AI experts predicting its emergence within this decade. The development of AGI promises to revolutionize industries by enabling machines to perform complex tasks without human intervention, potentially leading to significant economic and societal shifts.

2. PROGRESSION TOWARD ARTIFICIAL SUPERINTELLIGENCE (ASI):

ASI represents a level of intelligence that surpasses human capabilities in all aspects, including creativity, problem-solving, and emotional intelligence. The path from AGI to ASI is a subject of intense debate, with some AI researchers suggesting that once AGI is achieved, an intelligence explosion could rapidly lead to ASI. This progression would have profound implications, potentially transforming every facet of human civilization. However, it also raises critical ethical and existential questions that must be addressed by AI community proactively.

The year 2025 has been hailed as the year of AI agents, marking a significant evolution in artificial intelligence technology. While tools like ChatGPT and other large language models (LLMs) generative AI applications gained prominence for their ability to quickly and accurately respond to prompt engineering, the advent of AI agents has pushed the boundaries of what AI can achieve. These advanced AI systems, such as Copilot Studio, Operator in ChatGPT, and DeepSeek models are revolutionizing the field by not merely answering individual queries but by executing entire tasks (through AI agents) behind those queries. This shift signifies a monumental leap from simple conversational AI to sophisticated agents capable of performing comprehensive tasks autonomously. By leveraging the capabilities of AI agents, users can now delegate complex workflows and multifaceted operations, ensuring that these AI systems handle everything from initiation to completion with minimal human intervention. This evolution promises to streamline processes across various industries, enhancing efficiency and productivity. For instance, in healthcare, AI agents could manage patient data, schedule appointments, and even assist in diagnostic procedures. The focus in 2025 is on the transformative potential of AI agents, illustrating a future where AI handles complex tasks, thereby enabling humans to focus on more strategic and creative endeavors (Smith, 2025).

4. DEMOCRATIZATION AND COST REDUCTION IN AI DEVELOPMENT:

The recent emergence of DeepSeek, a Chinese AI company, has challenged the traditional paradigm of AI development. DeepSeek's open-source reasoning model rivals existing models but operates at a fraction of the cost and resource consumption. This breakthrough has significant implications for the AI industry, suggesting a shift towards more accessible and cost-effective AI development. The democratization of AI could lead to widespread adoption across various sectors, fostering innovation and competition. However, it also raises concerns about data center demands and the broader implications for AI accessibility and sustainability.

AI is increasingly becoming embedded in everyday applications, from personalized recommendations to autonomous vehicles. The next decade is expected to see deeper integration of AI into various aspects of daily life, enhancing convenience and efficiency. However, this ubiquity also necessitates robust discussions around privacy, security, and ethical use to ensure that AI technologies are deployed responsibly.

AI's Role in Shaping Society and the Economy

1. ECONOMIC TRANSFORMATION:

AI is poised to drive significant economic transformation by enhancing productivity, creating new markets, and disrupting existing business models. The automation of routine tasks can lead to cost savings and efficiency gains, while AI-driven insights can inform strategic decision-making. However, this transformation also poses challenges, including potential job displacement and the need for workforce reskilling.

2. Societal Impact:

The societal impact of AI is multifaceted, influencing areas such as healthcare, education, and social interactions. AI has the potential to improve healthcare outcomes through personalized treatment plans and predictive analytics. In education, AI can offer personalized learning experiences, catering to individual student needs. However, the pervasive use of AI also raises concerns about data privacy, algorithmic bias, and the digital divide, which must be addressed to ensure equitable benefits.

3. Ethical and Existential Considerations:

The advancement toward AGI and ASI brings forth ethical and existential considerations. Ensuring that AI systems align with human values and do not pose unintended risks is paramount. Discussions around AI ethics, governance, and control mechanisms are critical to prevent scenarios where AI actions could be detrimental to humanity.

Preparing for an AI-Driven Future

1. POLICY AND REGULATION:

Governments and regulatory bodies must establish frameworks that promote innovation while safeguarding public interests. This includes developing policies that address data privacy, security, and ethical AI deployment. International collaboration will be essential to create standardized regulations that manage the global implications of AI.

2. EDUCATION AND WORKFORCE DEVELOPMENT:

Preparing the workforce for an AI-driven future involves investing in education and training programs that equip individuals with relevant skills. Emphasis on STEM education, critical thinking, and adaptability will be crucial. Additionally, fostering interdisciplinary learning can help individuals understand the broader implications of AI and contribute to its responsible development.

3. PUBLIC ENGAGEMENT AND TRANSPARENCY:

Engaging the public in discussions about AI developments fosters transparency and trust. Providing accessible information about AI technologies, their benefits, and potential risks empowers individuals to make informed decisions and participate in shaping the future of AI.

4. ETHICAL AI DEVELOPMENT:

Developers and organizations must prioritize ethical considerations in AI design and deployment. This includes ensuring fairness, accountability, and transparency in AI systems. Implementing robust testing and validation processes can help mitigate biases and prevent unintended consequences.

In conclusion, the future of AI holds immense potential to drive progress and innovation. However, realizing this potential requires a balanced approach that anticipates challenges and proactively addresses ethical, societal, and economic considerations. By fostering collaboration among stakeholders, investing in education, and developing robust policies, society can navigate the complexities of an AI-driven future and harness its benefits for all.

Key Takeaways

1. **AGI and ASI** remain theoretical but are advancing rapidly, with DeepSeek accelerating AI democratization.

2. AI is set to **reshape economies and job markets**, necessitating new workforce skills.

3. **Ethical concerns** around AI must be addressed, particularly regarding bias, privacy, and misinformation.

4. Governments and businesses must **prepare regulations and policies** to ensure responsible AI development.

5. Individuals should **invest in AI literacy** to stay relevant in an AI-driven world.

Knowledge Check

1. What are the key differences between AGI and ASI?

2. How has DeepSeek influenced the AI development landscape?

3. What industries will be most impacted by AI in the next decade?

4. What are the potential risks of AI-driven financial markets?

5. What measures can governments take to regulate AI responsibly?

6. What is the difference between prompt engineering and AI agents?

Exercise

Scenario Analysis: Imagine it is 2035, and AGI has just been achieved. You are an AI policy advisor for a global organization. Write a **1-page proposal** outlining:

- The **opportunities** AGI presents for business and society.
- The **risks and ethical concerns** that must be mitigated.
- Three **policy recommendations** to ensure responsible AGI deployment.

REFERENCES

- Bostrom, N. (2014). *Superintelligence: Paths, Dangers, Strategies*. Oxford University Press.

- Domingos, P. (2015). *The Master Algorithm: How the Quest for the Ultimate Learning Machine Will Remake Our World*. Basic Books.

- Kurzweil, R. (2005). *The Singularity Is Near: When Humans Transcend Biology*. Penguin.

- OpenAI. (2023). "The Future of Artificial Intelligence." Retrieved from www.openai.com

- Smith, J. (2025). *The Rise of AI Agents: Transforming Industries and Workflows*. AI Journal.

- YouTube: *The Next 3 Years of AI: Why Even Experts Are Terrified* (https://www.youtube.com/watch?v=86GV5zhNA4g)

CONCLUSION: THE ROAD FORWARD IN AN AI-DRIVEN WORLD

Artificial Intelligence has woven itself into the fabric of modern life, reshaping industries, redefining jobs, and presenting new ethical and societal challenges. What once seemed like science fiction is now part of our daily routine assisting doctors in diagnosing diseases, powering autonomous vehicles, generating human-like text, and optimizing supply chains with unmatched efficiency.

But AI is more than just a tool for automation and efficiency; it is a transformative force that demands thoughtful engagement. Throughout this book, we have explored its foundations, applications, and implications— detailing the breakthroughs that have brought us here and the challenges that lie ahead.

Embracing the Potential, Acknowledging the Risks

AI is neither inherently good nor bad—it reflects the data, the algorithms, and, most importantly, the people who design and deploy it. While it holds the power to create economic growth, enhance decision-making, and unlock new forms of creativity, it also carries risks. Bias in algorithms, ethical dilemmas in automation, and the societal shifts that AI brings must be addressed with clear intention and responsibility.

As AI capabilities continue to evolve, so too must our frameworks for governance, transparency, and ethical use. Businesses must balance the pursuit of AI-driven efficiency with commitment to fairness and accountability. Governments must craft policies that encourage innovation while protecting fundamental rights. And individuals, whether as consumers, professionals, or policymakers, must take an active role in shaping AI's impact on society.

The Human-AI Partnership

Despite fears of machines replacing human intelligence, the future is not about humans *versus* AI—it's about humans *working with* AI. The most successful organizations and individuals will be those who embrace AI as an augmentation tool rather than a replacement. In business, AI can optimize strategies, but creativity and emotional intelligence remain uniquely human strengths. In medicine, AI can analyze vast datasets, but a doctor's intuition and empathy are irreplaceable. Across all sectors, AI will empower people to do more, think bigger, and solve problems in ways previously unimaginable.

Preparing for the Future

The AI-driven world will require continuous adaptation. Lifelong learning, digital literacy, and critical thinking will be more important than ever. Education systems must evolve to equip students with AI fluency, ethical reasoning, and critical thinking skills. Organizations must invest in their upskilling workforce to navigate the technological shifts ahead.

The key takeaway is this: AI is not an unstoppable force that will dictate our future. Rather, it is a tool that we must shape and guide. By staying informed, asking the right questions, and making responsible choices, we can ensure that AI serves humanity's best interests.

Final Thoughts

As we stand on the edge of an AI-powered future, the question is no longer *if* AI will transform society, but *how* we choose to direct its evolution. Will we use it to amplify our potential, solve pressing global challenges, and create a more equitable world? Or will we allow it to exacerbate existing inequalities and ethical dilemmas?

The future of AI is not just in the hands of scientists, engineers, or policymakers—it belongs to all of us. It is up to each of us to engage in conversation, advocate for responsible AI development, and ensure that these **thinking machines** work for the benefit of humanity.

The rapid advancement of AI and its large language model (LLM) tools is outpacing our ability to keep up. As we become familiar with one AI tool, another emerges, surprising us with its capabilities. Experts predict that 2025 will be the year of AI agents, but we cannot definitively say this will be the final milestone. The development of new AI tools will be driven by their utility and the problems they aim to solve. On one side, AI will address existing challenges and enhance the tasks users perform. On the other hand, a multitude of competitors, whose expertise transcends both physical and intellectual boundaries, are eager to explore uncharted territories and take calculated risks. This competition fuels innovation and accelerates the pace of technological advancements. As we witness these rapid developments, it is essential to appreciate the current technological marvels while remaining optimistic about future breakthroughs. Embracing this dynamic landscape allows us to experience the benefits of today's AI innovations and look forward to the next wave of transformative technologies. As AI continues to evolve, it will undoubtedly bring new opportunities and solutions, shaping the future in ways we cannot yet fully comprehend. What happens next is not determined by technology itself, but by the choices we make today.

Dr. Altaf Siddiqui

Dr. Altaf Siddiqui has over 20 years of experience in various IT disciplines. He began his training career as an adjunct professor of Computer Science and has trained approximately 10,000 IT professionals throughout his career. Altaf holds a master's degree in Computer Science and a Ph.D. in Educational Technology, where he invented an Instructional Modeling Language (IML).

He has held roles such as Senior IT Consultant, Architect, Assistant Director of Data Management, and Director of Training. Currently, he works as a Senior/Master Trainer for a multinational IT company.

Dr. Siddiqui teaches Java, Python, Statistics, Machine Learning/AI, Data Science, and Neuro GenAI, among other subjects. He has been a member of several professional organizations and advises IT organizations and technical strategic committees, including AECT, on emerging technologies. Additionally, he serves as the president of a Chamber of Commerce.

Dr. Siddiqui loves the outdoors. In summer, he enjoys fishing, and in winter, he goes skiing and hunting. He can be reached at Amer.Entps@gmail.com.

Greg Jameson

Greg Jameson is a recognized authority in leveraging artificial intelligence (AI) and ecommerce to drive business growth and innovation. With over three decades of experience at the forefront of technology, Greg has revolutionized how companies approach online sales, digital marketing, and AI integration. His groundbreaking work has empowered businesses of all sizes—from small startups to Fortune 500 corporations—to unlock new revenue streams and achieve measurable success.

As the author of several acclaimed books, including AI Advantage, Amazon's Dirty Little Secrets II: AI Edition, Make Magic Happen: The POWER of AI to Generate REAL Customers, and AI Chronicles, Greg delivers actionable strategies for businesses to stay ahead in the rapidly evolving digital landscape. His insights blend cutting-edge AI applications with proven ecommerce techniques, making him a sought-after consultant, speaker, and trainer.

Known as the "AI Architect for Business Growth," Greg brings unparalleled expertise in developing custom AI tools, enhancing corporate performance through training, and creating dynamic, personalized customer experiences. His AI Blueprint Builder Mastermind Program has been instrumental in helping businesses assess their readiness for AI implementation and develop actionable plans for sustainable growth.

Greg's contributions to the field have earned him prestigious accolades, including recognition on the Inc. 500 list, being named Colorado Small Business of the Year, and receiving the International Developer of the Year award. He combines this experience with a hands-on approach, ensuring his clients achieve results that exceed their expectations. Contact Greg at Greg@GregJameson.com.

www.ingramcontent.com/pod-product-compliance
Lightning Source LLC
Chambersburg PA
CBHW070941050326
40689CB00014B/3299